Repair and Upgrade
Your Own PC

Kenneth L. Hughes

Wordware Publishing, Inc.

Library of Congress Cataloging-in-Publication Data

Hughes, Kenneth L.
    Repair and upgrade your own PC / Kenneth L. Hughes.
      p. cm.
    Includes index.
    ISBN 1-55622-403-6
    1. Microcomputers--Maintenance and repair.   2. Microcomputers--
    Upgrading.   I. Title.
    TK7887.H84   1994
    621.39'16--dc20

                          93-45354
                               CIP

Copyright © 1994, Wordware Publishing, Inc.

All Rights Reserved

1506 Capital Avenue
Plano, Texas 75074

No part of this book may be reproduced in any form or by any means
without permission in writing from Wordware Publishing, Inc.

Printed in the United States of America

ISBN1-55622-403-6

10 9 8 7 6 5 4 3 2 1

9401

All inquiries for volume purchases of this book should be addressed to
Wordware Publishing, Inc., at the above address. Telephone inquiries may be
made by calling:

(214) 423-0090

Contents

Introduction
    Aims ix
    Organization x
    Knowledge Levels xiv
    Disclaimer xiv

Part One—Familiarization

Section 1-1—Overview 3
    Types of Personal Computers 3
    Failures 8
    Limitations of Repair 9
    Upgrade Versus Repair Decision 10
Section 1-2—Component Parts Primer 11
    Introduction 11
    Motherboard 12
    BIOS (Basic Input/Output System) 14
    Keyboard BIOS 15
    CMOS (Complimentary Metal Oxide Semiconductor) . . . 15
    CPU (Central Processing Unit) 15
    Memory Chips 15
    Switches 21
    Control Panel Connectors 23
    Power Supply 23
    Floppy Disk Drives 26
    Hard Disk Drives 27
    Floppy and Hard Disk Drive Controllers 30
    Adapter Cards 31
    Cables 38
    Speaker 40

Section 1-3—Peripherals Primer 42

    Keyboards 42

    Mice 43

    Digitizing Tablets 45

    Scanners 45

    Monitors 46

    Printers 48

    Plotters 49

    Modems 50

Section 1-4—Operating System 51

    Profile 51

    Loading DOS 52

    DOS After Startup 55

    Beyond the Basics 56

    Some DOS Problem Solving Commands 58

Part Two—Basic System Troubleshooting and Repairs

Section 2-1—Preview 63

    Ground Rules 63

    Proprietary Diagnostic and Disk Utility Programs 64

    Windows 3.1 Microsoft Diagnostic Utility 66

    Nonproprietary Diagnostic Programs 68

Section 2-2—Some Startup Problems and Immediate Responses . 71

    Symptoms 71

    Hardware 73

    Software 74

Section 2-3—Data and Disk Recovery 78

    Introduction 78

    Disk Protection 79

    Undeleting 81

    Unformatting 82

    Disk Repair 83

    Disk Recovery Services 85

Section 2-4—Disassembly Instructions 86

    Work Space 86

    Preparation 87

    Tools 87

    Disassembly 88

Section 2-5—Keyboards 92

    Overview 92

    Problems and Responses 93

    Preventive Maintenance 94

Section 2-6—Monitors and Video Cards 95

    Overview 95

    Problems and Responses 95

    Replacing a Monitor 97

    Replacing a Video Card 97

    Preventive Maintenance 98

Section 2-7—Power Supplies 99

    Overview 99

    Problems and Responses 99

    Power Supply Removal 100

    Power Supply Replacement 100

    Preventive Maintenance 101

Section 2-8—Memory 102

    Overview 102

    Problems and Responses 102

    Basic Responses 103

    Memory Removal 104

    Memory Insertion 104

    Preventive Maintenance 106

Section 2-9—Motherboards and the BIOS 107

    Overview 107

    Problems and Responses 108

    BIOS Removal 108

    BIOS Replacement 109

    Motherboard Removal 109

Motherboard Replacement 110
Preventive Maintenance 112

Section 2-10—Floppy Disk Drives 113
Overview 113
Problems and Responses 113
Cleaning Floppy Disk Drive Heads 115
Floppy Disk Drive Removal 115
Floppy Disk Drive Installation 116
Preventive Maintenance 117

Section 2-11—Hard Disk Drives 118
Overview 118
CHKDSK 119
Problems and Responses 119
Hard Disk Drive Removal 120
Hard Disk Drive Installation 121
Initialization 122
Formatting 123
Preventive Maintenance 125

Section 2-12—Adapter Cards 126
Overview 126
Problems and Responses 126
Adapter Card Removal 129
Adapter Card Installation 129
Preventive Maintenance 130

Section 2-13—Cables 131
Overview 131
Drive Cables 131
Control Panel Cables 132
Exterior Cables 132

Section 2-14—Reassembly and Testing 133
Assembly 133
Powering Up and Testing 133
Failed Boot 134

Part Three—Peripheral Troubleshooting and Repairs

Section 3-1—Mice 137
    Overview 137
    Problems and Responses 138
    Preventive Maintenance 138

Section 3-2—Digitizing Boards 139
    Overview 139
    Problems and Responses 139
    Preventive Maintenance 140

Section 3-3—Scanners 141
    Overview 141
    Problems and Responses 142
    Preventive Maintenance 142

Section 3-4—Printers 143
    Overview 143
    Problems and Responses 143
    Preventive Maintenance 144

Section 3-5—Plotters 145
    Overview 145
    Problems and Responses 146
    Preventive Maintenance 147

Section 3-6—Modems 148
    Overview 148
    Problems and Responses 149
    Preventive Maintenance 149

Part Four—Upgrades

Section 4-1—Overview 153
    Planning an Upgrade Configuration 153
    Upgrading Components 154
    Upgrading an XT to an AT 155
    Upgrading an AT-286 to an AT-386 or 486 157
    The Upgrade or "Bare-bones" Purchase Decision 158

Section 4-2—Adding or Upgrading Components Other Than
    Motherboards 159
  Memory 159
  Floppy Disk Drives 163
  Hard Disk Drives 164
  Disk Controller Card 166
  Power Supply 167
  Video Subsystem 168

Section 4-3—Setting Up a Hard Disk 169
  Initializing 169
  Formatting 170
  Directories and Files 172
  Loading the DOS Files 175
  Creating a CONFIG.SYS File 176
  Creating an AUTOEXEC.BAT File 176

Section 4-4—Upgrading an XT to an AT-286, 386, or 486 178
  Components and Parts to Order 178
  Component Removal 178
  Installing the Upgrade Components 180

Section 4-5—Upgrading an AT-286 to an AT-386 or 486 185
  Components and Parts to Order 186
  Component Removal 186
  Installing the Upgrade Components 187

Section 4-6—Configuring an Upgraded System 192
  Overview 192
  Buying Considerations 193

Appendix A—Prices 197
Appendix B—Typical I/O Addresses 200
Appendix C—Shareware and Public Domain Vendors
    and Organizations 202
Appendix D—Monitor Radiation 203
Glossary 205
Index 215

INTRODUCTION

AIMS

The aims of this book are to provide private and corporate users with knowledge and skills to the extent they are able to repair and/or upgrade their IBM-compatible PC, XT, or AT computer, either in order to effect economies, or for the purpose of self-interest and convenience. Because of the relatively larger number of AT machines in use today, greater emphasis is given to them than to PCs and XTs.

Do not be confused or concerned by the word "repair." As with most technological developments in this day and age, repairs invariably consist of replacing faulty components, and so it is with computers. Opening up a component and "tinkering" with it using pliers and screwdriver is a thing of the past. However, it is possible to repair a floppy or hard disk using software disk recovery tools, and you learn to do this in a later section.

The author believes that few repairs or upgrades can be satisfactorily performed without a clear understanding of the components being replaced or upgraded. Accordingly, Part One of this book is primarily a tutorial covering the hardware, the peripherals, and the disk operating system of a PC. You will benefit by studying the sections that deal with the component you suspect is faulty, or which you plan to upgrade.

DOS, the disk operating system, governs the running of applications, therefore a good understanding of it will help in diagnosing and fixing problems related to it and to application software, as well as making the installation of software upgrades easier.

Descriptions of components are supported by diagrams where appropriate. The diagrams are largely schematic, but have been used instead of photographs in order to provide improved clarity over photographs, which sometimes obscure detail. Screen captures of software utility programs are also used to illustrate some procedures.

For those who want in-depth knowledge beyond the need-to-know level, advanced information is supplied where appropriate under the heading of Beyond the Basics.

There is much to learn about the subject of computers; in fact, it is the author's experience that learning never seems to stop because of the continual technological progress that is being made. However, once the basics are mastered, it is not difficult for the average user to keep abreast of developments by regularly reading one of the better computer magazines. When you have absorbed the information contained in this book and finished the hands-on activities, you should have mastered the basics of personal computers, and never again will you need to have blind faith in the diagnosis and repair estimate of a service company.

Activities guide you through identifying and analyzing faults, carrying out repairs, and upgrading your PC. However, if your PC or any component is under warranty, do not attempt to carry out a repair; exercise your warranty rights with the original supplier.

ORGANIZATION

This book is organized into this introduction followed by four parts with each one containing sections—Part One familiarizes you with the components and operating system of your personal computer; Part Two covers basic system troubleshooting and repairs; Part Three covers peripheral troubleshooting and repairs; and Part Four embraces upgrades. Appendixes list tabulations and other information except for Appendix A - Prices. Because readers will not all have access to the same supply source of computer components, and because prices that are current at the time this book was written may differ greatly from those prevailing at the time you are reading this book, no attempt has been made to include them. However, because pricing may be important to you in making a repair or upgrade decision, you are urged to obtain a recent copy of Computer Shopper (available at book stores), or other sources of pricing, and complete the blanks in Appendix A. You should do this right after reading this book so that the information will be available to you when you have a problem and need to make the repair/upgrade decision. The procedure will also allow you to assemble names and locations of supply companies.

In order to save the upgrader having to frequently refer back to the repair sections of the book, procedures are generally given in full even if this has meant some duplication of text. Nevertheless, if you are an upgrader, you may benefit from reading Part One—Familiarization.

The program on the source diskette that comes with this book is used as a diagnostic training tool but, because it is public domain, you may use it freely, copying it to a hard disk if you wish.

The lists that follow record the information and activities presented in each section of this book.

Part One—Familiarization

Section 1-1—Overview: Types of personal computers, failures, limitations of repair, upgrade versus repair decision

Section 1-2—Component Parts Primer: Introduction, motherboard, BIOS, keyboard BIOS, CMOS, CPU, memory chips, switches, control panel connectors, power supply, floppy disk drives, hard disk drives, floppy and hard disk drive controllers, adapter cards, cables, speaker

Section 1-3—Peripherals Primer: Keyboards, mice, digitizing tablets, scanners, monitors, printers, plotters, modems

Section 1-4—Operating System: Profile, loading DOS, DOS after startup, beyond the basics, some DOS problem solving commands

Part Two—Basic System Troubleshooting and Repairs

Section 2-1—Preview: Ground rules, proprietary diagnostic and disk utility programs, Windows 3.1 Microsoft diagnostic utility, nonproprietary diagnostic programs

Section 2-2—Some Startup Problems and Immediate Responses: Symptoms, hardware, software

Section 2-3—Data and Disk Recovery: Introduction, disk protection, undeleting, unformatting, disk repair, disk recovery services

Section 2-4—Disassembly Instructions: Work space, preparation, tools, disassembly

Section 2-5—Keyboards: Overview, problems and responses, preventive maintenance

Section 2-6—Monitors and Video Cards: Overview, problems and responses, replacing a monitor, replacing a video card, preventive maintenance

Section 2-7—Power Supply: Overview, problems and responses, power supply removal, power supply replacement, preventive maintenance

Section 2-8—Memory: Overview, problems and responses, basic responses, memory removal, memory insertion, preventive maintenance

Section 2-9—Motherboards and the BIOS: Overview, problems and responses, BIOS removal, BIOS replacement, motherboard removal, motherboard replacement, preventive maintenance

Section 2-10—Floppy Disk Drives: Overview, problems and responses, cleaning floppy disk drive heads, floppy disk drive removal, floppy disk drive installation, preventive maintenance

Section 2-11—Hard Disk Drives: Overview, CHKDSK, problems and responses, hard disk drive removal, hard disk drive installation, initialization, formatting, preventive maintenance

Section 2-12—Adapter Cards: Overview, problems and responses, adapter card removal, adapter card installation, preventive maintenance

Section 2-13—Cables: Overview, drive cables, control panel cables, exterior cables

Section 2-14—Reassembly and Testing: Assembly, powering up and testing, failed boot

Part Three—Peripheral Troubleshooting and Repairs

Section 3-1—Mice: Overview, problems and responses, preventive maintenance

Section 3-2—Digitizing Boards: Overview, problems and responses, preventive maintenance

Section 3-3—Scanners: Overview, problems and responses, preventive maintenance

Section 3-4—Printers: Overview, problems and responses, preventive maintenance

Section 3-5—Plotters: Overview, problems and responses, preventive maintenance

Section 3-6—Modems: Overview, problems and responses, preventive maintenance

Part Four—Upgrades

Section 4-1—Overview: Planning an upgrade configuration, upgrading components, upgrading an XT to an AT, upgrading an AT-286 to an AT-386 or 486, the upgrade or "bare-bones" purchase decision

Section 4-2—Adding or Upgrading Components Other Than Motherboards: Memory, floppy disk drives, hard disk drives, disk controller card, power supply, video subsystem

Section 4-3—Setting Up a Hard Disk: Initializing, formatting, directories and files, loading the DOS files, creating a CONFIG.SYS file, creating an AUTOEXEC.BAT file

Section 4-4—Upgrading an XT to an AT-286, 386, or 486: Components and parts to order, component removal, installing the upgrade components

Section 4-5—Upgrading an AT-286 to an AT-386 or 486: Components and parts to order, component removal, installing the upgrade components

Section 4-6—Configuring an Upgraded System: Overview, buying considerations

KNOWLEDGE LEVELS

As with all "how to" books, the degree of ease with which you are able to repair or upgrade your PC will largely depend upon background experience. Nevertheless, there is nothing mysterious about a PC, and repairing or upgrading one usually involves no more than the relatively simple process of replacing a number of components in a logical order and connecting cables at the right places.

DISCLAIMER

Neither the author nor the publisher hold themselves in any way responsible for loss of data, or loss of income or other sources of reward as a result of such lost data, resulting from following any of the procedures detailed in this book, nor from loss of warranty if a warranty is still in force.

PART ONE
FAMILIARIZATION

Section 1-1

OVERVIEW

TYPES OF PERSONAL COMPUTERS

There are, of course, many makes and types of personal computers, but this book is only concerned with IBM PC-compatibles that operate on MS-DOS or equivalents such as PC-DOS, and which are IBM-PC hardware compatible. A personal computer that has IBM-PC compatibility will run any software that can be run on an IBM-PC, XT, or AT, and will accept any hardware that will function in an IBM-PC, XT, or AT such as circuit boards, power supplies, drives, etc. Nevertheless, we are only dealing with IBM-PC compatibles—clones of the PC—and there are numerous makes of such clones, all of different shapes and sizes.

You determine if your computer is IBM PC-compatible from the user's manual, where there should be a statement to that effect if it is truly compatible. You determine what your operating system is by typing VER (for version) at the DOS prompt in root, and the make and version of the operating system will be displayed providing it is MS-DOS compatible.

The main controlling hardware factor in determining IBM-PC compatibility is the design of the bus—essentially the information path from the CPU, but most often seen as the rigid conductor on the motherboard that accepts adapter cards. You will learn more about the bus in later sections. In modern PCs there can be three types of bus architecture: the standard bus that was used in the first IBM-PCs, the micro-channel in the IBM PS/2 line, and the EISA (Extended Industry Standard Architecture) which was the clone-manufacturer's response to IBM's micro-channel.

3

Micro-channel architecture (MCA) calls for physically smaller interface cards and uses a different technique to connect the cards than standard architecture. The MCA design also provides greatly improved functionality.

EISA is a design incorporating many of the improvements of MCA, but retaining physical compatibility with the standard bus.

DEVELOPMENT OF THE PC The first PCs had little memory, storage capacity, or clock speed. Later PCs became available with considerably more memory (1MB of which 640K was addressable), but no improvement in storage capacity or speed until the XT came into being. The XT was IBM's name for a PC with a hard drive and this was about the time when production of clones of the PC by other companies became a serious factor in the marketplace, and was when the term "IBM-compatible" seriously entered our vocabulary. The names PC, XT, and AT are registered to IBM, although the name PC is used indiscriminately to describe virtually any personal computer. This book will use those names, together with 286, 386, or 486 as appropriate, to refer to IBM-compatible personal computers.

Intel, the principal manufacturer of central processing units (CPUs), provided IBM with the 8088 series of processing chip that was the heart of their PC, and it was the design of this chip that determined the amount of memory the system could address, as well as controlling the speed of operation. As experience was gained, Intel found ways to add speed to their chip, but it was necessary for it to be a "second" speed, with the original 4.77MHz still being available on the chip. This new Intel chip was snatched up by clone manufacturers in order for them to produce what became known as a Turbo XT: a machine that could be boosted from a clock speed of 4.77MHz to 8.00MHz and more by keyboard command, and later from a control panel on the front of the computer case with a light emitting diode (LED) to indicate when the CPU was running in turbo mode.

Intel introduced several improved versions of the 8088 chip such as the 8086, 80C86, and the 80186, each offering an increase in either clock speed or bit-size (see Table 1-1/1). In addition to Intel, NEC has long produced CPUs, and more recently Cyrex Corporation and Advanced Micro Devices Inc. have entered the field.

MODEL	MAX SPEED (MHz)	INTERNAL DATA BUS (Size in Bits)	EXTERNAL DATA PATH (Size in Bits)	ADDRESSABLE MEMORY (MB)
8088	8	16	8	1
8086	8	16	16	1
80C86	8	16	16	1
80186	16	16	16	1
80286	20	16	16	16
80386SX	33	32	16	16
80386DX	40	32	32	4096
80486SX	40	32	16	16
80486DX	50	32	32	4096
80486DX2	66	32	32	4096

Table 1-1/1—Intel CPU Specifications

The next truly significant development on the PC's road to power was Intel's 80286 CPU which resulted in the first ATs. This was a major leap forward covering all facets of performance, and was the step that first brought the PC into serious competition with mini-computers and even older mainframes. The 80286 processing chip provided the advantages outlined in the list that follows:

- Clock speeds up to three times greater than 8088 speeds
- Ability to address up to 16MB of memory
- A 16-bit data-path
- Protected memory which prevents programs that use extended memory from exceeding the amount allocated by the CPU. Allocations are limited to 64K segments.

Improvements to Intel's 80286 CPU led to speeds of up to 20MHz, and with the introduction of the 80386 speeds shot up to 33MHz, then 40MHz, and 50MHz with the more recent 80486. Using a speed doubling technique, the 486DX is able to increase the speed of 33MHz CPUs to 66MHz and, no doubt, even higher speeds will have been attained by the time this book is in print. The 386 and 486 processors have the further advantage of a 32-bit data path.

The 80386 processing chip was a major refinement of the somewhat cruder 80286, and provided the advantages outlined in the list that follows.

- Ability to address up to 4096MB (over 4 gigabytes) of memory
- A 32-bit data-path
- The 386 protected memory mode prevents programs that use extended memory from exceeding the amount allocated by the CPU, but allocations can be of any size up to the available total of 4 gigabytes (gb).

The SX series might be considered as the "poor man's" 386, being no more than a 386 CPU installed in a modified 286 board. These hybrids provide for a 32-bit internal data-bus which hypes up the internal computing speed, but retains the restriction of the 286's 16-bit external data path. For more information on this subject, read Beyond The Basics that follows.

BEYOND THE BASICS Like all computers, the PC operates on the binary system ("bi" meaning "two") and the two are "on" and "off." In other words, the basis of a CPU is an ultra-high speed switch that makes and breaks an electrical circuit. Each switching action is called a bit, with ON represented by 1, and OFF by 0. Using an 8-bit process, characters can be represented by a series of eight bits. (The eight bits of a character make up one "byte.") For example, when the D key is pressed on the keyboard, the CPU is switched on and off eight times in the sequence shown in Figure 1-1/1. Other circuitry is then able to hold the information in random memory until needed, store it on a disk, convert the signals to video representation which can be seen on the screen, or convert the signals to printer language for hard copy reproduction.

Character	Binary Representation
D	0 1 0 0 0 1 0 0
O	0 1 0 0 1 1 1 1
S	0 1 0 1 0 0 1 1

Figure 1-1/1—Binary system

Data Paths The Intel 8088 family of CPUs have an 8-bit data path: to all intents and purposes an 8-wire path along which eight bits of information can travel in parallel, resulting in the movement of one full byte at a time. The eight paths represent width, therefore the CPU is said to have an 8-bit bus. The Intel 80286 chip has a 16-bit bus which permits the movement of two bytes at a time, significantly speeding up processing time. Advertisements specifying a computer as being 8-bit or 16-bit are referring to the bus width and not expansion slot size.

The address bus is distinctly different from the data bus, being the width of the wire path that carries addressing information to specify a location for data in the memory. Each wire carries a single bit of information that is a single digit in the address, and because a computer works on the binary numbering principle, a 2-bit bus would provide only four addresses (00, 01, 10, and 11), and a 3-bit bus eight addresses (000, 001, 010, 011, 100, 101, 110, 111). The 8088 CPU, which has a 20-bit address bus, provides 1,048,576 addresses which are the equivalent of a megabyte, thus the maximum memory addressable by the 8088 CPU is 1MB. XT computers with the 8088 CPU have sockets for 1MB of RAM and there would be no purpose in adding more. The 80286 CPU has a 24-bit address bus providing 16,777,216 (16MB) addresses and, therefore, is able to address 16 megabytes of memory. The true 80386 or 80486 with 32-bit address busses provide 4,294,967,296 (4096MB) addresses and could handle 4,096 megabytes of memory although, of course, sockets are not normally provided for anything like this amount of memory.

CPU Speeds CPU speed is measured in megahertz (MHz), previously described as CPS (cycles per second) but recently changed in honor of Heinrich Rudolph Hertz for his experimental work in electromagnetism during the late nineteenth century. Thus, a CPU with a clock speed of 16MHz is completing 16 million cycles per second and, depending on the efficiency of the CPU, using perhaps 5 cycles to execute a single instruction (i.e., one step in a batch of steps that instructs the CPU to carry out a task). Because of the varying efficiency of CPUs, the measure of cycles per second does not give a true indication of processing speed, thus the term MIPS (millions of instructions per second) is growing in usage. Using the above figures of 16MHz and 5-cycle efficiency, the computer would be rated at 3.2 MIPS. Relative to the very fast 486 CPUs, even the "mind boggling" 3.2 MIPS is slow, but when compared with the original PC of only about ten years ago, the mind truly does have difficulty in making a realistic comparison.

FAILURES

On the whole, you should find that the modern PC gives trouble-free operation for many years, except for problems created by you, the user, and by the environment.

A saying often heard in computer circles is: "Garbage in, garbage out," meaning, of course, that the PC makes mistakes only when instructed to do so by the user—even if inadvertently. Most times, incorrect instructions will do no more than cause temporary frustration, but in some cases they can lead to more serious trouble, such as a major loss of data.

The most likely physical trouble you may expect will be centered on your floppy drives and your power supply (the unit in the computer, not the current from a wall outlet). These components, together with your hard drive, are the only ones that have moving mechanical parts, prone to wear. A hard drive is a sealed unit and is, therefore, less likely to fail than a floppy drive which is exposed to dust and moisture as well as being subjected to the physical action of diskette insertion and removal.

Your power supply is multifunctional with one of the functions being to act as a cooling system. The fan in the power supply sucks air into your PC through vents and other openings including the mouth of a floppy disk drive. The air passes around the electronic devices within the computer case (some of which generate considerable heat) before being pulled through vents on the inside walls of the power supply and then exhausted through other vents at the back of the case. Pollutants in the air will cause more damage to the fan and other moving parts in the power supply than to stationary electronic parts within the PC. Furthermore, by the time the moving air enters the power supply it will have gathered heat. Environmental considerations are, therefore, of considerable importance in extending the life of your floppy disk drives and your power supply and, of course, in reducing the risk of failures.

The power supply in your PC is also the first component to receive an electrical current from a power source. But even with the shielding provided by a surge protection device, electrical current in some areas of the country is so "dirty" that fluctuations get through to your PC, and it is the power supply that takes the brunt.

Clearly, you can extend the life of your PC by protecting it from "dirty" electrical current by using an efficient voltage regulator, and by maintaining an unpolluted environment within the temperature range recommended in the PC's user manual. By following these practices, and by doing your best to avoid the "garbage in" syndrome, you will also save yourself from considerable frustration. But when frustration does strike—as is almost inevitable—the guidance given in this book should make it short lived, allowing you to quickly get back into the pleasures of smooth computing.

LIMITATIONS OF REPAIR

Since the average PC-user has neither the tools nor the skills to replace parts that are soldered to major components, you are likely to be limited to replacing only those which are removable without special tools, and the major components themselves. The following is a list of those items which are also described in some detail in later sections.

- Power supply
- Floppy disk drive
- Floppy drive controller card
- Hard drive
- Hard drive controller card
- Floppy/hard drive controller card
- Drive ribbon cables
- Interface (or expansion) cards (or boards)
- Motherboard (or mainboard, or system board)
- Memory chips or modules
- CPU chips
- Numeric coprocessor chip (if installed)
- Keyboard BIOS chip
- Jumpers
- Battery (if installed)
- Speaker

UPGRADE VERSUS REPAIR DECISION

More than anything else, the age and model of your PC will be a determining factor in deciding whether to repair or upgrade in the event of a major failure. Obviously, if your ten-year-old original PC is adequate for the work you do on it, and if the failure is caused by nothing worse than, say, a floppy disk drive controller cable, your decision will be to repair. But if a strike of lightning "fries" your power supply and motherboard, upgrade becomes a logical choice.

When a problem does occur, and when you sit there staring glumly at the blank monitor of your dead computer, don't despair. Think positively, make use of the diagnostic techniques explained in this book, identify the problem, calculate the cost of repair by using as a guide the figures you will enter in Appendix A, and then make the upgrade comparison.

Some decisions will be more obvious than others. For example, if your old, slow, too small, 20MB hard disk drive has totally crashed, don't send it out for repair unless you absolutely must make an attempt to save the data on it. Not only might the repair shop tell you it cannot be fixed, but you might get a hefty bill from them just for investigating. Obtain a copy of the Computer Shopper magazine or another source of suppliers, study it carefully, follow the guidance given in Section 4-6, then order an appropriate new 40MB drive. Next, install it and set it up by following the instructions in Section 2-11.

Another example would be the failure of a low-density disk drive in use on a basic PC or XT. Instead of replacing the drive, buy a high-density one for just a few dollars more, then for an additional expenditure of plus or minus $150.00, you upgrade to a 286 machine and get into the mainstream so far as new application software is concerned where, in many cases, an AT machine is a must.

Study the situation carefully before reaching a decision, balancing the limitations of your budget against the benefits you will receive, and do not forget to factor in the increased life that upgrading may give to your PC.

Section 1-2

COMPONENT PARTS PRIMER

INTRODUCTION

No two PCs of different makes are the same under the cover. However, like humans who don't look alike but have the same parts, once you recognize the component parts in one PC you will recognize them in another. For example, the motherboard and the adapter cards have as a base a thin, rigid, laminated sheet of material, usually green or brown in color. As a rule, one side will be almost covered with chips, switches, jumpers, transistors, connectors, and other devices, and the other side will show the lines of printed circuits and the soldered ends of the connecting pins of the chips, etc.

Some adapter cards consist of two cards (known as "piggy-back" cards) separated by 0.25-inch to 0.50-inch spacers. Such cards allow for a greater number of electronic devices to be fitted to the card, particularly memory.

In a desktop PC, the motherboard is always flat on the floor of the computer case, while the adapter cards stand on edge with their connectors fitting into the rigid bus of the motherboard. In a tower or mini-tower, the motherboard is vertical and the adapter cards are horizontal. The only other major components in both are the power supply—a large, aluminum box located at the rear of the case, and the drives, which are located at the front of the case.

With the cover removed, the principal components are easily identified: they are the motherboard, the memory chips or modules, the power supply, the adapter cards, the floppy disk drives, the hard disk drives, and the cabling. Figure 1-2/1 that follows shows a typical layout for an AT-286 PC using DIP memory.

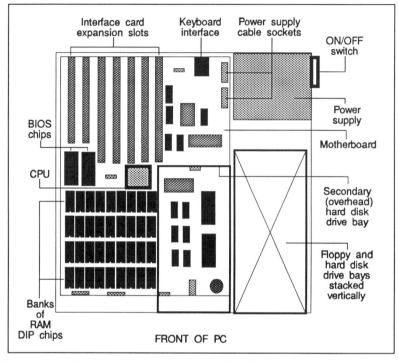

Figure 1-2/1—Under the cover of a typical AT-286

MOTHERBOARD

The motherboard, which may be multilayered, incorporates printed circuits that link together all the electronic devices such as transistors, chips, connectors, etc., that are located on the board. The connectors (or expansion slots) for adapter cards are connected to a parallel BUS that can accept a number of electrical circuits. A standard bus is shown at Figure 1-2/2.

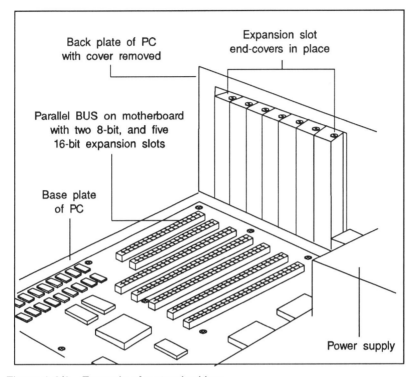

Back plate of PC
with cover removed

Expansion slot
end-covers in place

Parallel BUS on motherboard
with two 8-bit, and five
16-bit expansion slots

Base plate
of PC

Power supply

Figure 1-2/2—Example of a standard bus

Although motherboards have similar parts, they are often not the same size, which is why the base plate in a computer case offers a variety of locating and securing positions. Most motherboards are located on the base plate of the case by plastic stand-offs described in Figures 1-2/3 and 1-2/4.

13

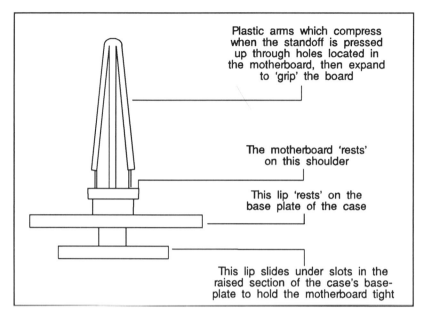

Figure 1-2/3—Motherboard plastic stand-off

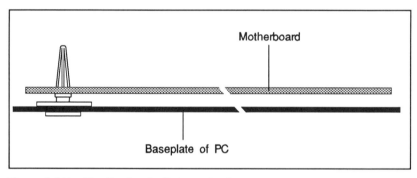

Figure 1-2/4—Plastic stand-off shown in place

BIOS (Basic Input/Output System)

Usually supplied as a pair and often marked "ODD" and "EVEN," the BIOS contains the preprogrammed instructions that make the PC active after switching on (known as powering up or "booting," although booting more accurately refers to the stage when DOS takes over).

With ATs, the BIOS runs an internal diagnostics procedure and, at first power-up after an upgrade, it invariably finds that the actual (new) configuration does not compare with the default configuration that was "read" into the CMOS chip at the last setup. When the BIOS finds system configuration changes, a message will be displayed requesting you to enter the setup program in order to record the new configuration in CMOS.

The functions of the important BIOS chips are also covered in Section 1-4.

KEYBOARD BIOS

A keyboard BIOS chip contains preprogrammed instructions for keyboard operations and is "matched" with the main BIOS in an AT. In an XT, the chip is in the keyboard.

CMOS (Complimentary Metal Oxide Semiconductor)

You program a CMOS memory chip to store the system configuration such as time and date, memory, disk drives, and monitor information, but for this information to be retained when the PC is not in use it must be backed up by a small internal battery. (The CMOS chip is not found on XTs which use switches and jumpers to set configuration.)

CPU (Central Processing Unit)

The most important chip is the CPU, or microprocessor, the heart of the system once it has been powered up. This chip interprets and routes the information that is fed into the PC. Information (instructions) can be input from a keyboard, a mouse, a digitizing tablet, a modem, a scanner, or a disk, and even by voice on a system appropriately configured. Output can be to monitor, disk, printer, plotter, modem, or any networked computer.

MEMORY CHIPS

Of the many other chips that assist in processing, analyzing, filtering, and routing the computer's two-way flow of information, the best known are likely to be the memory chips which provide your PC with Random Accessible Memory (RAM): a volatile memory that only becomes active when the computer is turned on, and disappears like mist evaporating when the computer is turned off. RAM chips are usually located on the motherboard although, with some makes of PCs, they are located on an add-on board. Notches on chips or modules and on sockets guide you in installing them in the correct alignment; indented dots replace notches on some DIP chips. Memory chips are available in the following types and sizes, with a variety of speeds—speed being the rate in nanoseconds (ns) at which they will handle two-way traffic.

DIP (Dual Inline Package) DIP are individual chips that "plug" directly into sockets on the main board in banks of nine as shown in Figure 1-2/5. DIP chips are available in memory sizes of 64K, 256K, or 1MB, and nine chips are usually required to provide an equivalent amount of memory. However, there are a few DIP configurations other than nine.

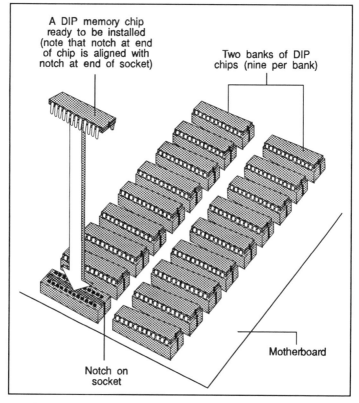

Figure 1-2/5—Two banks of DIP memory chips

SIMM (Single Inline Memory Module) A bank of nine miniaturized chips on a mini-card with a strip connector that "plugs" into a special socket on the main board of an AT, as shown at Figure 1-2/6. These chips are available in 256K, 1MB, or 4MB sizes.

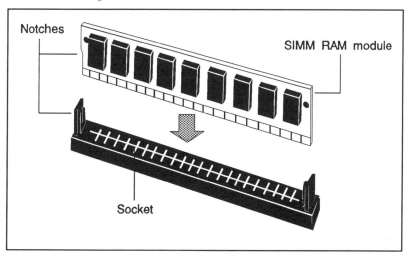

Figure 1-2/6—SIMM module

SIP (Single Inline Package) Similar to SIMMs except they use a pin-style connector instead of ribbon.

SIMM and SIP are relatively new technology and, because they are much easier to install, they are likely to supplant DIP with SIMM being predominant.

BEYOND THE BASICS The information that follows should be of relevance to you if your interest in computers goes beyond seeing them simply as a useful tool.

Random Accessible Memory Technological advances made in recent years in the production of low-cost, miniaturized memory devices are the prime reason for the high speed, flexibility, and popularity of today's PC.

Most machines today are delivered with at least 640K of memory, and often with 1MB or more. Although we tend to refer casually to a megabyte of memory today and do not necessarily think of it as being very adequate for modern application programs, mainframes of two decades ago served hundreds of terminals with only 1MB of memory.

17

The PC uses RAM for program instruction storage and data storage. The great advantage of computer memory as compared with a recording tape is the "random" feature. The contents of each storage cell can be directly accessed through the chip's connectors, whereas a tape must be moved to the part containing the information to be recovered.

Two of the several attributes of a memory chip are size and speed. Size is specified in kilobytes and speed in nanoseconds. Speed relates to the time required by a chip to accept an instruction following receipt of the previous one, and the chip's speed will directly influence system performance. Cheaper, slow chips (above 100ns) delay processor activity because of the time lapses between acceptance of instructions by the memory. This delay in processor activity is called a wait-state, and there can be more than one wait-state in a PC. The number of wait-states needed to match memory chip speed can be set on an AT, usually by jumpered switches. When memory was relatively expensive it was acceptable to operate a system below the processor's optimum speed by using slower, cheaper chips and inserting wait-states—providing applications were not so complex as to cause unacceptable delays in execution. However, when the price difference between fast and slow memory chips is only a few dollars, your AT should be operated with memory that permits no wait-states.

The most common configurations for RAM contain banks of nine DIP chips, and these chips can be of different values. For example, they might total 64K, 256K, or 1MB, but in each case the memory is contained in only eight of the chips, with the ninth being a "controller" or "parity" chip that keeps track of the total memory in the other eight. Memory can become corrupted from a number of causes and, when discovered by the ninth chip, the processor is advised through an interrupt called the Non-Maskable Interrupt and a "parity error" message is displayed. An interrupt is no more than a temporary suspension of processor activity, but in most cases of memory problems the suspension becomes permanent and the system must be powered down and restarted after the fault has been corrected.

There are a considerable number of parity error messages, and they vary according to the make of the BIOS. Most PC user manuals list error messages, giving a description of the cause of the message and the remedial action to take.

Types and Modes of Memory There are three types of memory: conventional, expanded, and extended; and three memory modes: real, protected, and 386 enhanced. Conventional memory consists of the first megabyte, of which 640K is the base memory for user programs and data, 128K is for on-screen display of text and graphics, another 128K is ROM (read only memory) for the use of adapter cards, and a final 128K for ROM in the system BIOS. Figure 1-2/7 illustrates memory maps for the XT and the AT.

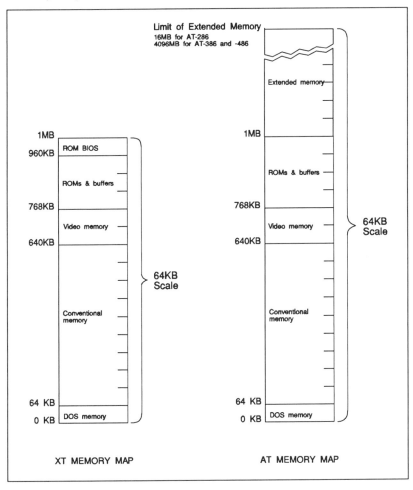

Figure 1-2/7—Memory maps

If the video adapter does not require the full 128K reserved for it, there are ways to make it available for use by DOS; otherwise, so far as the user is concerned, versions of DOS prior to MS-DOS 5.0 can only work with the first 640K. When restricted to this first 640K, the computer is in the "real mode."

The term "real mode" came into being when the 80286 CPU was designed and, in order to allow for compatibility, an 8088 mode (real mode) was built in. However, compatibility was obliged to be 100% and, from the RAM point of view, the new 286 CPU merely operated like a very fast XT, with no other benefits and no way to make use of memory above one megabyte.

As application programs became larger, needing more memory, efforts were made to solve the problem by Lotus, Intel, and Microsoft. These three computer companies developed a technique known as "bank switching" which increases the apparent address space without increasing the number of hardware address lines and made possible the use of "expanded" memory. Expanded memory uses a fixed block of address space in the first megabyte of memory to serve as a "window" onto a much larger array of memory which does not have an address in the 8088 memory map. This technique became known as the Lotus-Intel-Microsoft Expanded Memory Specification (LIM EMS) and it enabled software programs that recognized it to draw on memory above one megabyte a "page" at a time. The original EMS specification provided up to 8MB of bank switchable memory, but this was revised in version 4.0 of the EMS to provide a maximum of 32 megabytes.

Fortunately, users were not stuck for too long with this useful but somewhat cumbersome technique. With the advent of Windows 3.0, DOS 5.0, and other software, memory above the first megabyte became accessible as extended memory when the 80286 processor was running in its natural mode, the Virtual Protected Mode.

The 386 enhanced mode, which includes the 386SX, 386, and 486, can be used with appropriate software to create "virtual" memory by using a free portion of the hard disk. Virtual memory must be recreated each time a computer is turned on.

SWITCHES

A motherboard may have either dipswitches or jumpers (which act as switches), or both. Dipswitches are in banks of up to eight or more, as can be jumpers, although they are usually found in smaller groupings. Dipswitches are miniature switches, a bank of eight being about one inch long. Jumpers, shown in Figure 1-2/8, have caps which are about a quarter of an inch in height.

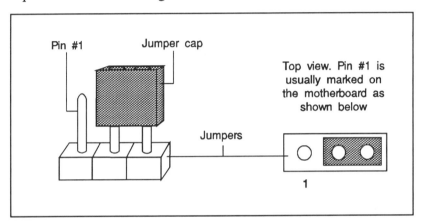

Figure 1-2/8—Jumpers

Dipswitches and jumpers are used for setting variables such as:

- Color or monochrome video
- Type of RAM
- Number of memory banks used
- Amount of memory
- Processor speed
- Wait states.

Typical dipswitch and jumper positions are shown in Figure 1-2/9.

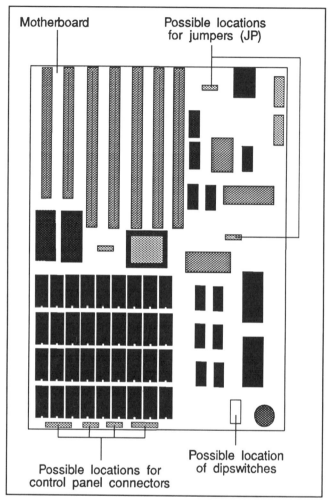

Figure 1-2/9—Typical dipswitch & jumper positions

If there is no cap on a jumper, or if the cap is only on one pin, then the switch is not closed. If a jumper has three pins, the center pin is common, and which two of the remaining pins are capped (shorted) will determine, for example, if color video or monochrome is selected.

CONTROL PANEL CONNECTORS

Uncapped jumpers are also used to make cable connections to the motherboard from the control panel. These connections between the motherboard and the control panel are for the purpose of activating the following:

- Speaker
- Power LED (light emitting diode)
- Key lock
- Reset switch
- Speed switch (turbo)
- Turbo LED

The user manual that comes with a motherboard should provide details of all dipswitch and jumper selections, as well as control panel cable connections. Jumpers are usually referred to as JP followed by a number, and control panel cable jumpers by J followed by a number.

An uncapped jumper is provided for an external battery connection in the event the "built-in" battery fails. A built-in battery can be replaced but it involves soldering the connections, which can be a difficult task. An external battery is only external to the motherboard and, when used, is usually attached to the side of the power supply by a Velcro pad.

POWER SUPPLY

The power supply converts standard 115-volt 60Hz AC current to a 5-volt DC current acceptable to the microcircuits and components of a computer, and to a 12-volt DC current for the motors driving the fan and the disk drives.

The power supply in the PC itself has a connection to a regular power source, but this should be via a surge protector to protect the delicate electronic circuitry and chips against current fluctuations which, at the least, might garble data or, at the worst, burn out electronic units, losing all data. Better than a surge protector is an Uninterruptible Power Supply (UPS) which contains a battery capable of running the system for about 10 minutes so that the operator can save data and power down in an orderly manner in the event of a power outage.

Power supplies vary in both ratings and design, with wattage ratings varying from 150 to 230, and designs varying to suit the various cases that are available. With an AT-286 or 386, a power supply with a minimum of 200 watts is desirable. Buying a power supply by mail order often results in the wrong design being received, frustrating to say the least, and it is usually better to take your old power supply to your local computer store and have them supply one of the same design, even if at greater expense. The design variations usually relate to height and length, power cable socket position, and main switch location, although there are other more radical changes with some computer case designs such as those with very small "footprints" and some types of mini-tower.

With most PCs, the power supply fits into the back right-hand corner of the.case, with the ON/OFF switch to the right, and the slots in the base plate of the power supply sliding over the lips protruding from the bottom of the case. The power supply is then secured to the back plate of the case using screws.

The power supply has two types of cable connector. The first type supplies power to the motherboard using two sets of six cables each, usually marked P8 and P9. These cables plug into sockets on the motherboard. If the identification numbers are not clear, locate the connector with an orange wire first, so that the orange wire is closest to the rear of the computer case as shown in Figure 1-2/10. The other type of cable connector, which provides power to the disk drives, has four wires and there are usually four sets of them. Extensions are available for the drive cables if they are of inadequate length to reach the drives.

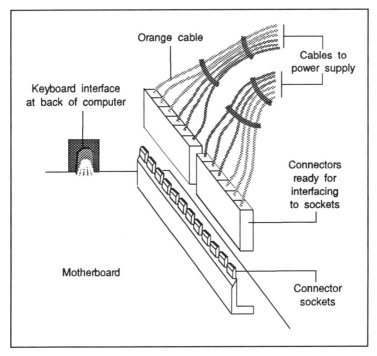

Figure 1-2/10—Illustration of power supply connections to motherboard

A male socket and a female socket are located at the rear of the power supply. The male one accepts the supplied computer power cable for bringing power from the wall outlet or surge suppresser to the computer. The female socket is useful for taking power to a peripheral, particularly the monitor, but a cable for the female socket is not supplied, although some makes of monitor are supplied with a power cable that fits the socket. However, most peripherals are supplied with power cables for connection directly to a wall outlet or surge protector, thus the second, female socket is rarely used.

CAUTIONS

1. Ensure that the voltage selector (if fitted) is set to the correct voltage before connecting to an electrical outlet.

2. The warning on a power supply case not to open the case should be heeded. The case contains a large capacitor that retains electricity and can induce a bad shock.

25

Power cables should be connected to a surge protector or an uninterruptible power supply, and not directly into wall outlets.

FLOPPY DISK DRIVES

A floppy disk drive is a device with a magnetic head that can write and/or read information to and from a floppy diskette. Most ATs and XTs are limited to a drive that accepts 5.25-inch diskettes with maximum storage capacity of 360K, or 3.5-inch diskettes of 720K capacity. (For the convenience of quick mental math, we say that 1K equals 1,000 bytes, although in fact it equals 1,024 bytes.) While 286 through 486 machines can also be installed with the 360K and 720K drives, they are the only ones that can use 5.25-inch/1.2 megabyte (MB) and 3.5-inch/1.44MB drives where, for quick math, one MB equals 1,000,000 bytes. More recently, 3.5-inch/2.88MB drives have become available for machines using MS-DOS 5.0 or 6.0.

Up to two floppy disk drives may be installed, designated A and B, and within the limitations of the computer model, any combination can be installed.

Since drive bays on most desktop machines are designed for 5.25-inch drives, adapters are available for 3.5-inch drives so that they may be housed in 5.25-inch bays.

BEYOND THE BASICS The factory-set configuration of new floppy disk drives is usually for a single floppy disk drive setup, and installation is simple. However, floppy disk drives do have the following configuration devices:

- Drive-select jumper
- Terminating resister

Drive-Select Jumper A disk controller card and the system's drive subsystem recognize a drive by a unique single-digit number, with numbers commencing at 0 (zero), and is not to be confused with the DOS method of recognizing a drive, which is with single letters commencing with A. Although there is some inconsistency in the design and location of the jumper, making it difficult to offer clear advice, the default jumper setting is nearly always acceptable; but, should you experience problems, consult the manual supplied with your PC or the drive.

Terminating Resistor Most floppy disk drives have a terminating resistor, but not all do. If you are in doubt, you must refer to the drive's user manual if you have it, or to an experienced person. When two drives are installed, using a single ribbon cable with two drive connectors, the drive at the end of the cable must always have the terminating resistor in place if one is installed, even if it is the only drive. In the case of a second drive connected from within the length of the cable, the terminating resistor if installed must be removed. A simplified explanation of how a drive not provided with a removable terminating resistor functions is that it automatically signals the CPU as to whether it is A or B.

HARD DISK DRIVES

Hard disk drives also have magnetic heads to read or write data, but most do not have a removable disk. The disks, or platters, are fixed (usually more than one) in separated vertical layers, as shown in Figure 1-2/11, and their storage capacity ranges from 10MB to several hundred MBs.

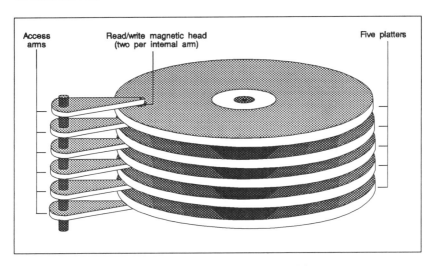

Figure 1-2/11—Schematic view of inside a hard disk drive

20MB, 30MB, or 40MB drives are the sizes most found in PCs, although larger drive sizes are becoming common. Hard drives are not accessible from outside the computer but they have an indicator light that shows when the drive is in use. They are desirable because of their high storage capacity, because application programs too large to be run off floppy drives can be loaded directly onto them, and because they are able to transfer information bits very much faster than a floppy drive. However, like all electronic devices, hard drives can malfunction, and when they do there is a risk that stored data may be destroyed. Therefore, the stored information from hard drives should be copied (backed up) regularly onto floppy diskettes or tapes.

Care should be taken not to jar a disk drive (hard or floppy) by jolting a computer while it is in use; otherwise, the heads (two per platter) that read data may strike the disks and cause damage resulting in loss of data or even total destruction.

Most modern hard disks have an auto-parking device that keeps the heads away from the disks when the computer is not in use; otherwise, a DOS disk parking command should be used before powering down.

Whereas each floppy disk must be formatted before use, most hard disk drives must be initialized (low-level formatted) as well as formatted. Initializing prepares a hard disk for formatting. Formatting refers to procedures normally carried out using the DOS software and other specialized software. Formatting organizes a magnetic disk to receive data in a specific format.

BEYOND THE BASICS The following information covers most features of hard disk drives.

Size Differing makes and models of hard disk drives result in several physical sizes. For PCs there are 3.5-inch and 5.25-inch widths, and full- or half-heights. In older drives, height was largely determined by the number of vertically stacked platters, but with modern miniaturization techniques height is less significant. The number of platters influences the total storage capacity of a hard disk, which is the other measurement of size. A half-height disk is most often used in a modern PC, and it measures about 1.5 inches in height. Installation of a 3.5-inch drive in computer cases with 5.25-inch drive bays requires an adapter kit in order for it to fit.

The platters of a hard disk store data on both sides on a number of tracks. Two tracks in corresponding positions on each side of all the platters is called a cylinder.

28

Configuration Devices Hard disks also have drive-select jumpers and terminating resistors, usually mounted on the logic board at the bottom of the drive, and they perform the same functions as they do on a floppy disk drive.

Speed Hard disks are considerably faster than floppy disks, with speed being measured in two ways: access time and transfer rate. Access time is the average time taken for the reading heads to move from one cylinder to the next, while transfer rate is the speed at which the drive can send data to the motherboard.

Interfaces An interface matches the output of one device with the input of another device. Among the different types of interface, or data encoding schemes, are MFM (Modified Frequency Modulation), RLL (Run Length Limited), ESDI (Enhanced Small Disk Interface), SCSI (Small Computer System Interface), and IDE (Integrated Drive Electronics). An advantage of the RLL interface is that a disk can be formatted to have half as many tracks again compared with most other interfaces, thereby giving 50% increase in storage capacity. However, unless drive and controller are properly matched and are of high quality, periodic data loss is a real possibility. Advantages of the IDE interface are its very low cost and the fact that the disk is preinitialized. You will realize that because of the sensitive interrelationship between a drive and its controller it is essential for them to be properly matched. The SCSI interface allows other devices to be connected to it all at the same time; devices such as a CD-ROM, printer, scanner, etc.

Interleave Specifications Each track on a platter is divided into sectors, much like the slices of a pie, with the sectors numbered consecutively upwards from "1." As the platter spins at high speed, the head reads a sector and transmits the data to the motherboard and is then ready for the next sector. Unfortunately, sector "2" has already passed and the head must wait for all the other sectors (up to 17, or even 26) to pass before "2" comes round again. Interleaving renumbers sectors on a disk in an order selected to suit the transfer rate of the drive, so that the next sector due to be read is there when the head is ready. Drives formatted with a 1:1 interleave can transmit data at rates from 500 to 1,000 K/sec as compared with 130 to 300 at a 4:1 interleave. If speed is important, use a drive and controller that will permit 1:1 interleaving.

FLOPPY AND HARD DISK DRIVE CONTROLLERS

Disk drives need controllers. Controllers can be in the form of adapter cards or, in the case of floppy drives only, they may be an integral part of the motherboard. In the latter case, if a hard drive is installed, a hard drive controller will also be required. If the motherboard does not have floppy drive control capabilities, then a floppy drive controller card must be installed. With an XT, if a hard drive is installed, it requires a separate controller card, whereas an AT can use a combination floppy/hard drive controller card.

Figure 1-2/12 illustrates a full-length (16-bit) card designed to control two floppy and two hard drives. If designed for floppies only, the card would be half-length and would have a single 34-pin socket and no 20-pin sockets.

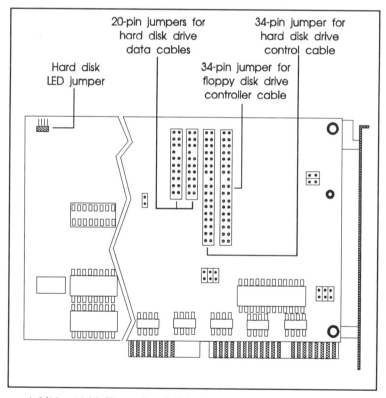

Figure 1-2/12—16-bit Floppy/hard disk drive controller

Some controller cards have their own BIOS chip with a program incorporated for formatting hard disks. Informative booklets are usually provided with such cards, and they provide step-by-step initializing instructions. IBM computers come with an initializing program called "IBM Advanced Diagnostics," but IBM-compatible computers do not have such a program and, therefore, other software is used. Typically, such programs might be:

- Programs supplied with the hard disk drive
- Proprietary programs ("Speedstor," for example)
- Programs built into the BIOS setup utility
- The DOS DEBUG program.

Most hard disks are initialized using different sets of fundamental parameters (the drive interface) that relate to specific types of controllers such as MFM, RLL, ESDI, SCSI, or IDE, which were described under the heading Hard Disk Drives in this section. Controllers and hard drives are best purchased together in order to avoid conflict with the drive interface. (A floppy disk drive can be managed by any floppy/hard controller regardless of the hard drive interface.)

ADAPTER CARDS

An adapter card (expansion board) is a printed circuit board fitted with electronic components. One end may be fitted with a connector (called a port) designed to accept a cable from an externally connected, or peripheral, device. The card installs into a BUS expansion slot on the motherboard, with the port exposed through a slot at the back of the computer as shown in Figure 1-2/13. For a computer to operate it must have two adapter cards: a video adapter for connection to a monitor, and a drive controller for connection to a floppy disk drive (although in some designs, the display and disk drive circuits of these cards are built into the motherboard, eliminating the need for separate cards).

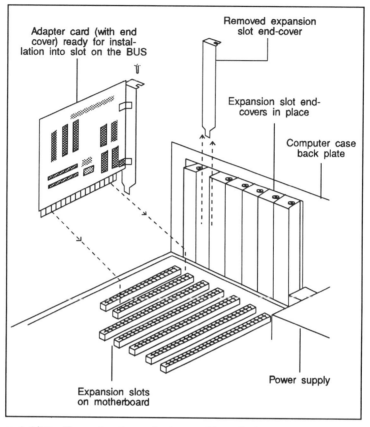

Figure 1-2/13—Example of an adapter card installation

Adapter cards are also needed for:

- Bus-mouse
- Disk drives (hard and floppy)
- External serial devices (modems, printers, and mice)
- Extra printer ports
- Internal modems
- Joy sticks for games
- Mainframe connections
- Networking
- Plotters
- Printers
- RAM in excess of motherboard maximum

- Scanners
- Speed cards
- Video adapter.

Surprisingly, adapter cards are seldom identified with a printed name and it is necessary to learn how to distinguish one from another. Generally, recognition is by the type of interface on the card or the type of port connector. For example, a disk controller card has rows of exposed pins that match the connector on the ribbon cable, and a bus-mouse card has a port that is unique to the connector at the end of the mouse cable. The list that follows contains a selection of video, parallel, and serial ports with a description of their use.

- Female with 9 pins in two rows. On its own it is likely to be a network port; with a female port of 25 pins in two rows it is likely to be a monochrome video/parallel printer port; with a single RCA connector it is likely to be a CGA video port; with two RCA connectors it is likely to be an EGA port.
- Female with 15 pins in three rows. VGA port.
- Female with 25 pins in two rows. Parallel port for a printer or other device.
- Male with 9 pins in two rows. Serial (communications) port, maybe with a 25-pin parallel port on the same card.
- Male with 25 pins in two rows. Serial (communications) port.

The more adapter cards and ports you install on your PC, the greater the likelihood of experiencing trouble because they require memory addresses, I/O addresses, DMA channels, or interrupts (IRQs). These four requirements are covered more fully in the following list.

- Memory Addresses—Your CPU must know at all times where it is storing information, and these locations are called addresses. Each address is a register that stores one byte of information. Some cards such as hard disk drive controllers, video adapters, and network cards require some memory in the course of their activities. In order to avoid memory clashes, fixed memory addresses are allocated for these tasks and they are described using the hexadecimal system (the letters A through F and the numbers 0 through 9). This memory is known as reserved memory and it is read only memory (ROM) to prevent it from being altered, an action that would result in confusion to say the least. There is only a limited amount of reserved memory available which, therefore, limits the number of cards that can be installed that require such memory.

- I/O Addresses—Any card that inputs or outputs information needs an I/O address, as do some electronic devices such as the keyboard controller on an AT, or the peripheral controller on an XT. A list of typical I/O addresses is given at Appendix B. Switches and jumpers on many I/O adapter cards allow you to set the address.

- DMA Channels—Direct memory access is a time saver. Four channels on an XT, and four more on an AT, are provided for use. The first three are permanently allocated: memory refresh, bisynchronous communication, and floppy disk. DMA channels allow the CPU to be bypassed when transferring "routine" information to RAM.

- IRQs—I/O devices use an IRQ to interrupt and stop the CPU when it is working with another application so that an input or output instruction can be handled promptly. XTs have eight interrupt lines and one interrupt controller. ATs have fifteen with two controllers. Figure 1-2/14 is a captured Windows 3.1 Microsoft diagnostic utility screen showing IRQ information for an AT. (See Section 2-1 for information about this Windows 3.1 utility.)

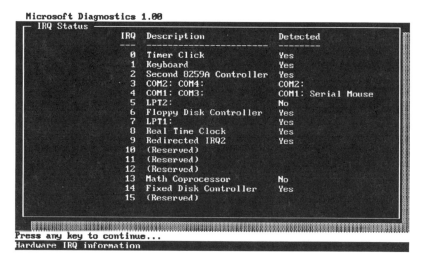

Figure 1-2/14—IRQ information for an AT

VIDEO CARDS The video card is the major player in the series of events that convert the touch of a keyboard or mouse button into activity on the monitor screen. The most simple and lowest cost video card is a nongraphics monochrome that produces characters only in green, amber, or white. Next in line, illustrated in Figure 1-2/15, is the monochrome graphics card (often called a "Hercules" graphics card after the name of a manufacturer) which will produce both characters and graphics on a monochrome monitor. These cards have ports for a 9-pin monitor cable and a 25-pin parallel printer cable. (Up to three parallel printer ports may be installed in a PC.)

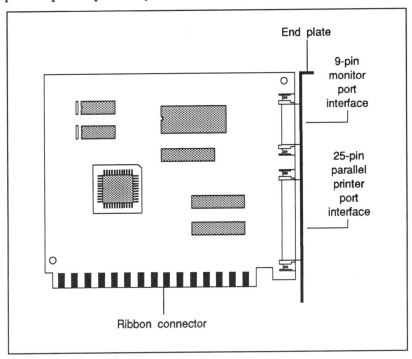

Figure 1-2/15—Typical 8-bit monographics card

Going to color brings forth some confusion in the terminology applied to the various cards that are available. One of the early color cards (and monitor) is called CGA (Color Graphics Adapter), but this card (as with the simplest monochrome card) offers inferior resolution. Progressing to the EGA (Enhanced Graphics Adapter), resolution is improved to 640 x 350 pixels. Next in line is the VGA (Video Graphics Array) card, with 8-bit versions offering 640 x 480 resolution, and

16-bit Super VGA cards going as high as 1024 x 768. Video cards for the larger screens used for DTP or CAD applications can provide resolutions up to 1250 x 1250 and beyond.

The number of colors that could be controlled with the earlier color graphics cards was very limited, but the modern VGA cards can provide from 16 to 256 colors, while the specialist cards for DTP and CAD go up to literally millions of colors.

Many video cards have memory chips installed in order to enhance resolution, increase the number of colors displayed, and speed up screen refresh time. Provision is sometimes made on the card for more memory chips to be added.

Most of the higher end color video cards have a single 15-pin port; others may also have a 9-pin port to enable the card to be used in the monochrome mode. None of these cards have printer ports, making it necessary for a specific printer card or a multi-I/O card to be installed. Figure 1-2/16 illustrates a typical middle-range VGA card.

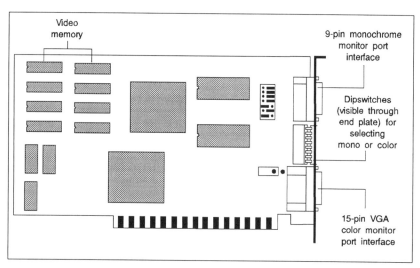

Figure 1-2/16—Typical VGA card

MULTI-I/O CARD   The reader will recall from earlier discussion on BIOS chips that the "IO" letters mean "input/output." A multi-I/O card is an adapter card that provides extra ports for both the input and output of data. Figure 1-2/17 shows an I/O card with a game port and a parallel printer port. The function of the game port is to provide an interface for the type of connector found on "joy sticks," which are used for controlling video games.

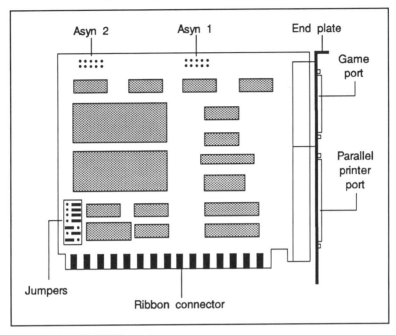

Figure 1-2/17—Multi-I/O card

Switches, which may be jumpers, allow the printer port to be designated "LPT1," "LPT2," or "LPT3" (DOS reserved names, with "LPT" being a contraction of local printer).

Other ports for communication are provided on a separate end plate, with each port having a 10-pin ribbon cable exiting from the back of the port. The other ends of the cables terminate with 10-pin connectors that interface with the 10-pin jumpers shown in Figure 1-2/17 as "Asyn 1" and "Asyn 2." These names refer to asynchronous communication ports which are better known as COM1 or COM2 (DOS reserved names that are contractions of "communication"). Most multi-I/O card kits include these two ports and their cables together with full instructions for configuring the ports if for any reason the default settings are not acceptable.

CABLES

There are several types of cable in a PC: six individually colored ones from the power supply to the main board; four individually colored ones from the power supply to the disk drives; ribbon cables from the disk controller adapter card to the disk drives; mini-ribbon cables between Input/Output (I/O) adapter cards and communication ports; and lightweight colored cables between the main board and external buttons and indicator lights on the control panel.

DISK DRIVE RIBBON CABLES Ribbon cables interface the drives to the controller card. Although there are several different designs, we are only interested in the three types which are in common use in IBM-compatible AT computers. They are:

- 34-pin controller ribbon cable for up to two floppy disk drives
- 34-pin controller ribbon cable for up to two hard disk drives
- 20-pin data ribbon cables for each hard disk drive.

Figure 1-2/18 is an illustration of a 34-pin cable for two floppy drives. The 34 wires that are soldered to the 34 pins in each of the connectors are embedded in the plastic ribbon cable, and the illustration shows that a section of the cable that houses wires 10 through 16 has been slit open and twisted before entering the first floppy drive connector.

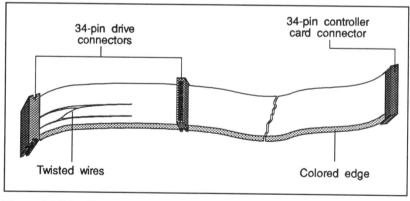

Figure 1-2/18—Floppy disk drive 34-pin ribbon cable

The twisting technique in a ribbon cable is required when two drives are used and it becomes necessary for the disk controller to be able to address both drives individually, rather than as a pair. However, a single drive will function using either of the connectors on this cable—twisted or not twisted. Cables with only one floppy drive connector are available, and they do not have the twisted section.

With a 34-pin cable for two hard drives, the twist takes place at wires 19 through 25. Thus the different cables can be easily recognized by the position of the twist relative to the colored edge strip, which is always on the same side. A single hard drive may also use this type of cable.

20-pin cables with a single connector at each end are for hard disk drives only, and each hard disk drive requires one of these cables.

20-pin and 34-pin hard disk drive connectors interface with the J1 and J2 strips on your hard disk drive, as shown in Figure 1-2/19.

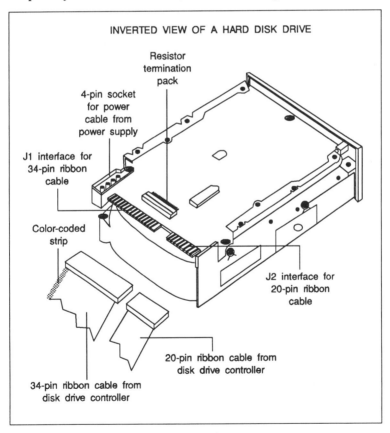

INVERTED VIEW OF A HARD DISK DRIVE

Resistor termination pack

4-pin socket for power cable from power supply

J1 interface for 34-pin ribbon cable

Color-coded strip

J2 interface for 20-pin ribbon cable

20-pin ribbon cable from disk drive controller

34-pin ribbon cable from disk drive controller

Figure 1-2/19—Hard disk drive cable interfaces

The connectors at the other end of the ribbon cables interface with pin jumpers, which are shown in Figure 1-2/12 in this section.

34-pin floppy disk drive connectors interface with J1-type strips at the back of the drive. The connectors at the other end of the cables interface with pin jumpers which were also shown at Figure 1-2/12.

As with all jumpers, pin #1 is so marked on the board or card (see Figure 1-2/8 in this section) and, when interfacing a ribbon cable, the position of the colored edge should correspond with pin #1.

In the case of the drive connectors, there is often a slot toward one side of the strip jumper and a bridge toward one side of the connector, making it impossible to interface the wrong way. With the controller connectors, if the jumper pins on the card are vertical (as shown at Figure 1-2/12 in this section), pin #1 is invariably at the top of the card, and with cards where the jumpers are horizontal, pin #1 is invariably toward the front of the computer when the card is installed.

SPEAKER

A speaker is not only required to give beep codes if the boot fails, but also for signaling information in application programs, particularly in respect of illegal keyboard commands.

The speaker is usually located in a plastic holder affixed to the computer case (see Figure 1-2/20).

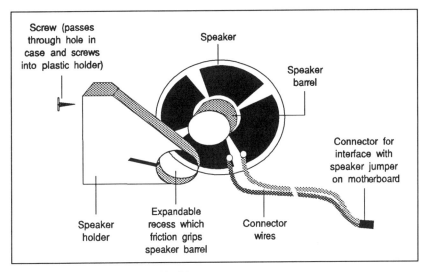

Figure 1-2/20—Speaker and holder

The barrel of the speaker presses into the expandable recess in the holder, which grips it tightly; then the holder is screwed to the wall of the computer case and the connecting wires are interfaced to the appropriate jumper on the motherboard.

In addition to the hole in the base of the holder, there is a small locating peg that fits into a prepared hole on one of the front left walls of the computer case. When in place, the holder will project off the wall.

The most common positions for the speaker are either off the front wall of the case, just to the left of the adapter card guides on the cage that protects the back of the control panel LEDs and buttons, or inside the cage, parallel with the front of the case and projecting off the left wall of the cage.

41

Section 1-3

PERIPHERALS PRIMER

Basically, peripherals include any connected equipment not housed inside the computer; however, this book only covers those peripherals normally supplied or used with a PC. Examples with connection information follow.

KEYBOARDS

The two most common types of keyboard available are the 84-key for PCs and XTs and the 101-key for ATs, with the principal difference being that on the 84-key board there are no independent scrolling keys. In some older boards, the F (function) keys may be found grouped on the left side instead of being in a line across the top of the board.

Keyboards require differing configurations to function with XT and AT PCs, and most modern keyboards are switchable, either by automatic sensing or manual control as shown in Figure 1-3/1.

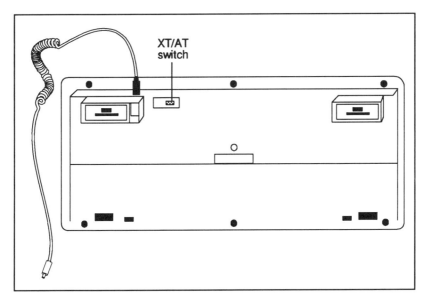

Figure 1-3/1—View of underside of a typical keyboard

Keyboards use a spiral cable with a 5-pin connector that fits directly to the main board through a round port, most times at the back of the computer.

Except for top-name keyboards such as IBM, Compaq, etc., most keyboards supplied with IBM-compatible PCs are assembled with the intent for them never to be disassembled. However, the keys can often be eased off for replacement or cleaning without removing the cover by carefully using a fine bladed screwdriver. Underneath the keys there is often a membrane protecting the printed circuit board housed in the case. The action of pressing a key completes a circuit on the board and sends a signal to the computer.

MICE

Used as alternatives (but not as replacements) to keyboards to input commands to the computer, these peripherals are connected by cable to a serial communications port, or in the case of a bus-mouse they are interfaced to a unique adapter card.

Most mouse bodies house a small ball which projects below the base. The ball turns as the mouse is moved causing internal rollers also to move and send signals to the monitor via the computer. These signals cause the mouse cursor to move on the monitor screen. A track ball works the same way except the ball is moved with a finger or thumb. Track balls can be flat-based to sit on a desk and manipulated by hand from above, clipped to the side of a laptop or notebook computer, or held in the palm of the hand with the thumb operating the ball. Figure 1-3/2 that follows is an example of the hand-held type.

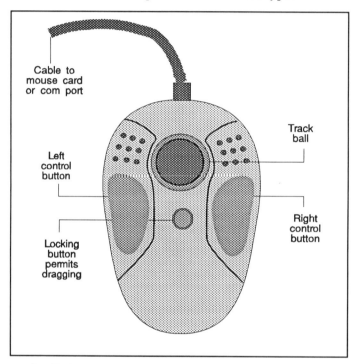

Figure 1-3/2—Typical hand-held track ball mouse

Buttons on any type of mouse complete a circuit when clicked. On a two- or three-button mouse, clicking the left button makes a selection or, when held down, allows the cursor to be dragged. The other buttons are generally for user-defined functions or for specific functions defined by application software.

There are several new designs now available such as the pen-mouse, but the principle of operation remains the same.

Cordless mice are also available, with the instructional signals being actually transmitted from mouse to adapter board.

DIGITIZING TABLETS

A digitizing tablet, generally used with a computer aided design (CAD) software program with output to a plotter, consists of a square or rectangular board with electronic sensors below the surface, and a stylus. Both are so wired as to permit a connection when the stylus (used like a drawing pencil) touches the board. As the stylus is moved across the board, it activates a series of sensors which are interpreted as cursor movement on the screen. The board is matched to the screen, and diagonal stylus movement from one corner of the board to another will result in cursor movement between the same relative screen corners. Lifting the stylus off one position on the board and placing it on another will cause the cursor to jump from one relative position to the other on the screen.

Various refinements have been introduced to both boards and stylus, allowing the user to make selections with the stylus both on the screen and on a coded strip across the top of the board.

Digitizer boards are connected by a shielded cable to a serial port and must be configured for both the type of computer and the software program to be used. Configuration is usually accomplished by setting rows of dipswitches located at the top backside of the board.

The stylus cable interfaces into the board, and the board itself is powered via a voltage regulating device that plugs into a power source.

SCANNERS

A scanner directs a band of light at printed characters or designs and measures the amount reflected back. The reflected light is recorded in dots, and the resolution of the recorded image will depend upon the "dots per inch" (dpi) attributes of the scanner. Any shades between black and white will be recorded in gray scales. The light band moves over the print (or vice versa) until the complete page has been scanned and the results sent via cable to the scanner adapter card where graphics or OCR software complete the interpretation.

Graphics software brings a "bit-mapped" image to the screen at the same dpi resolution as the scanner, although some graphics software is able to enhance the image to an apparent higher resolution.

Optical Character Recognition (OCR) software "reads" the bit-mapped image of scanned characters one at a time, defining them as specific letters by making comparisons with a selection of fonts held in memory. OCR tends only to be accurate when well-defined characters are scanned.

Other recognition software takes a more intelligent approach by applying rules to characters until definition becomes apparent. For example, an upper case F is recognized because it has one vertical and two upper horizontals open to the right. Recognition of an upper case P would commence in the same way but would end with the horizontals closed to the right. This type of software is more accurate and more expensive.

Scanned character software is able to format the completed scan (file) so that it can be imported into a word processing application program. Correction of misread characters can then be accomplished by spell-checking and proofing.

The modern scanner is available in hand-held models which roll over the media being scanned; desk models which accept 8.5-inch media through rollers; and flatbed models where the media is laid on a glass plate and a hinged cover is closed over it, like a copier.

Color scanners are available that can bring a full-colored picture to the screen.

Scanners are connected by cable to a port on a scanner adapter card.

MONITORS

There are probably more monitor makes and models than any other peripheral, so many in fact that to cover them adequately would call for a complete book. What follows is a summary of a monitor's salient features.

HOW THEY WORK A monitor depends upon a video card (also called video adapter or display adapter) to send it signals: alphanumeric when the card is in character mode, or defined pixels when in the graphics mode. A pixel is one illuminated dot on the screen. The video card retains in its memory (video cards have memory chips) every pixel on the screen and instructs the monitor which ones are to be illuminated. The monitor scans the video card frequently and rapidly, obeying instantly the continually changing instructions to illuminate pixels. The two units are known as the video subsystem.

BEYOND THE BASICS An electron beam in the monitor scans each line of pixels on the back of the screen horizontally, starting at the top left and then working down the screen from left to right. When it receives an instruction from the video card to illuminate a pixel, it projects an electron which causes the phosphor of the pixel to glow momentarily. In a color monitor, each pixel contains a dot of each primary color, therefore not only must the monitor be more complex (and more expensive), but the video card must be capable of issuing many more instructions than it does for a single color display. It must also be able to illuminate more than one dot of color in a pixel at a time in order to make other colors, or partially illuminate a dot(s) of color in a pixel in order to produce shades of a color. Again, the more complex, the more expensive, and price continues to rise for both color monitors and video cards with increases in resolution, i.e., the number of scanning lines per screen and the number of pixels per line.

COLOR OR MONOCHROME With nearly all cases of private ownership, price is the ruling factor. The resolution of a relatively low cost monochrome monitor is invariably better than the resolution of the cheapest color monitor, and even then the price difference is marked in favor of monochrome. If color is essential, then for the sake of your eyes, go for the highest resolution monitor and video card you can afford, and be aware that the most expensive color monitor will not necessarily provide high resolution if matched with a cheap video card.

RESOLUTION Compare monitor resolution with a photograph reproduced in a newspaper. View both through a magnifying glass and you will see they are made up with dots. The dots on the monitor screen are the pixels (picture elements), and resolution varies from a screen display of 640 x 200 pixels through 1664 x 1200 pixels. Another way to define resolution is by dot pitch, which relates to the way color dots of phosphor on the screen are lit up. Dot pitch ranges from a low of about .50mm to a high of .25mm. Unless you have an absolute need for color, the most economically effective combination is a monochrome (black and white) VGA monitor controlled by a VGA or Super VGA video card.

47

CONNECTIONS Monitors use a shielded cable with a connector where the pin count varies according to the type of monitor. The connector interfaces to a port on the video adapter card which projects through one of the slots at the back of the computer. Simple monochrome video cards usually also have a printer port.

PRINTERS

Like monitors, there are an immense number of printers on the market, but they define more easily into four types: the laser printer, the impact printer, the dot matrix printer, and the ink-jet printer.

LASER PRINTERS A laser printer is a form of computerized office copier. An electrostatically charged drum attracts a fine coating of black powder (toner), then a computer driven laser beam discharges areas of the drum causing the toner to fall away. The remaining toner is rolled on to a sheet of paper and then heat-fused to create a printed page. With 300 dpi (dots per inch) resolution and better, silent operation, together with speed and simplicity of use, the laser is a first choice if it can be afforded.

IMPACT PRINTERS These printers are basically computer driven typewriters, using a daisy wheel or thimble head to press ink from a tape onto paper. They tend to be noisy, slow machines without graphics capability, but they provide high print resolution.

DOT MATRIX PRINTERS The print heads on these machines have a vertical row of 9, 16, or 24 wires (or pins), and they print a character in a series of sections. For example, to print an uppercase T, several of the top wires strike the inked tape repeatedly as the head moves to the right across the paper to form the left arm of the crossbar of the character. When it is time for the vertical part of the character to be printed, all of the wires project until the vertical of the character is printed, and then the lower ones retract again leaving the top ones projecting to print the right arm of the crossbar. Because of their method of printing, more wires mean better resolution. They are affordable printers with choices of resolution by using fewer wires to allow for fast drafting, or all the wires for slower, but ncar-letter-quality printing. They are also capable of fair quality graphics reproduction and are less noisy than an impact printer but much noisier than a laser printer. Some dot matrix printers that can be adapted for color use a three-colored ribbon.

INK-JET PRINTERS   An alternative when a laser is too expensive and dot matrix resolution inadequate, these printers, which can give resolutions up to 300 dpi, do not have an inked tape but squirt accurately measured jets of ink onto the paper. They are quiet and reasonably fast. Some ink-jet printers use a water-based ink which is, therefore, not waterproof, and a printed page or envelope can become disfigured if exposed to water. Color versions are available at higher prices.

CONNECTIONS   Printers use a shielded serial cable or a parallel cable which may or may not be shielded. A parallel cable permits the flow of eight data bytes in line abreast, whereas in a serial cable the flow is one bit after another. Therefore, parallel data communication is faster and is preferred. The cable connector interfaces with a port on the video card, on a special printer card, or on a multifunction I/O card.

PLOTTERS

The key features of plotters are the size of media they can accept, speed and accuracy of operation, and the number of pens they can control. Media sizes range from 8.5-inch x 11-inch sheets, usually on desktop machines, and up to rolls of 36-inch width on long-bed pedestal machines. Plotters usually have full-length, power-driven rollers set in the bed of the machine and the media lies on these rollers. Other narrow spring-loaded rollers hold the media firmly in place. When the long roller is rotated by instructions from the CAD application software, the media is moved backwards or forwards under the pen. A pen holder, located above the roller on a transverse arm, is moved laterally on instructions from the program, thus high-speed movement in two directions allows even the finest detail to be plotted quite rapidly. A schematic representation of a long-bed plotter is shown in Figure 1-3/3.

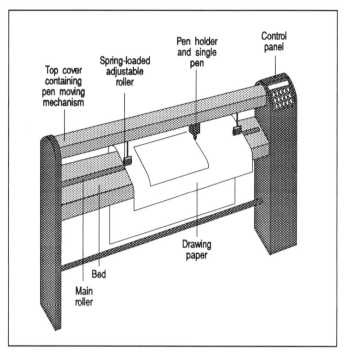

Figure 1-3/3—Representation of a long-bed plotter

Advanced plotters have an automatic pen changer so that color can be varied on command from the computer. Connectivity is by shielded cable that interfaces to a serial port; the cables may be serial, RS-232, or custom. RS-232 is supposed to be a standard, however, different manufacturers tend to come up with different specifications making the cable one to be avoided if possible.

MODEMS

An internal modem resides on an adapter card which has a jack for a telephone line connection accessible through one of the rear slots of the computer. An external modem connects by cable to a communications (serial) port at the back of the computer. The telephone line connection goes directly to a jack in the external modem.

The speed at which a modem can transmit data is called the 'baud' rate. A modem with a rate of 1200 baud is transmitting data at roughly 1200 bits per second.

Section 1-4
OPERATING SYSTEM

PROFILE

The most common operating system in use on IBM-compatible PCs is the one we deal with in this book, the Microsoft Disk Operating System (MS-DOS) in one of its several versions. Generally, the oldest version in use is 3.*, while the most common in use is probably 4.*, although the momentous upgrade provided by 5.0 may have put it in the top slot for the time being. However, the recently released version 6.0 is reported to have already sold over 5 million copies and looks to be the real winner.

The main advantage of 3.* over 4.* was the ability of 4.* to make a single partition on a hard drive, virtually regardless of size, thereby eliminating the need under 3.* to have a large storage capacity hard disk divided into several partitions named C, D, E, etc.

The greatest advantages of version 5.0 are memory handling, text editing, and utility tools. Improved memory handling gives the user access to areas of previously wasted memory between 640K and 1MB. Improved editing provides a straightforward text editor in addition to the old Edlin line editor. And the new utility tools include one which allows you to undelete a deleted file.

Among the new features of 6.0 are is its ability to link PCs and to share resources between them, to move files from one drive or directory to another, a disk defragmentation utility, the Microsoft System Diagnostics utility, and a virus safety utility.

DOS means different things to different people. Some use it only as the means to execute the commands they type on the keyboard; others, who enter their application programs via a shell with a menu, seldom make use of DOS; and programmers use DOS as an interface to disk, directory, and file functions.

PC-DOS, provided with "true-blue" IBM PCs, is IBM's implementation of DOS, while MS-DOS is Microsoft's. The two are almost 100% functionally equivalent, and the two companies make ongoing efforts to keep it so as either one develops a newer version. However, IBM has recently turned to an entirely new operating system which they have named OS/2; somewhat like a combined form of DOS and Windows.

LOADING DOS

When a PC is switched on, built-in routines prepare the system to accept DOS. In the case of 286, 386, and 486 machines, details of the computer's BIOS (Basic Input/Output System) are displayed on the monitor and an opportunity is given the user to enter setup in order to alter the system settings stored in the BIOS chip. Next, the startup routines "look" at drive A to see if DOS is waiting to be loaded. If DOS is not there, the BIOS looks for it at other installed drives. If DOS is not found, either a cursor blinks under the last displayed line on the monitor until DOS is provided, or a message is displayed asking for a DOS disk.

If a bootable hard disk (usually drive C) is not installed, a DOS boot diskette must be inserted in drive A prior to booting so that when the BIOS looks at drive A it will find DOS, activate the disk drive, and read DOS into memory. If a hard disk containing DOS is installed, it is not necessary to insert a DOS boot diskette, since the BIOS will pass over drive A and find DOS when it looks at drive C.

To help understand how DOS functions, visualize it loading in three separate stages as shown in Figure 1-4/1.

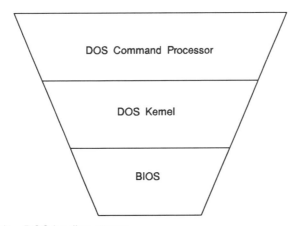

Figure 1-4/1—DOS loading stages

Every computer is supplied with the previously referred to set of routines programmed into the BIOS chip. Some routines are more elegant than others; the original PC routines were simplistic, while modern ATs can be complex, but each time you switch on your computer, the last action of the BIOS routine is to look for a boot record on a disk. The boot record is contained in the first sector of any bootable disk and, when found, it initiates the bootstrap program (hence the expression "booting a computer"). Incidentally, the object of the routines always looking at drive A first, is to make it possible for you to boot from a diskette in the event of hard disk failure.

The bootstrap program makes use of the input/output routines found in the read only memory (ROM) of the BIOS chip together with the hidden file IO.SYS to create a space in random accessible memory (RAM) to handle input and output. By communicating with the routines in ROM, DOS translates the information into a format the input/output devices are able to understand. With some devices such as mice and scanners, a DEVICE=nnn entry may be required in the CONFIG.SYS file, with "nnn" being the device name. The hidden file IO.SYS is one of two hidden files which, for example, are referred to in the display of information that follows execution of the DOS command CHKDSK.

The DOS kernel, or program section as it is sometimes called, is created during the starting procedure by the file MSDOS.SYS (the other hidden file) which is read into memory. The kernel controls the functions shown in the following list.

- File management (create, delete, edit)
- Directory management (make, remove, alter)
- Writing (to screen, disk, or printer)

The command processor carries out your commands by using the file COMMAND.COM. Consisting of three sections named startup, transient, and resident, the command processor is the key to user control of the computer; without it you cannot function.

The startup section has the task of executing the commands in the AUTOEXEC.BAT file and, as soon as the procedure is finished, the startup section is removed in order to free memory for other usage.

The complete sequence from the start to the end of DOS startup is shown schematically in Figure 1-4/2.

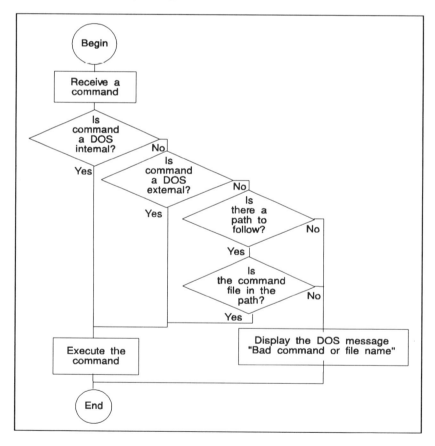

Figure 1-4/2—DOS startup

DOS AFTER STARTUP

The transient section of DOS is so named because many application programs overwrite it, and when the application program is terminated the resident section, which is held in memory at all times, reloads the transient section; a vital action because the transient section holds all the DOS internal commands which are given in the following list.

BREAK	DATE	PATH	TIME
CHDIR	DEL	PROMPT	TYPE
CLS	DIR	REN	VER
COPY	ERASE	RMDIR	VERIFY
CTTY	MKDIR	SET	VOL

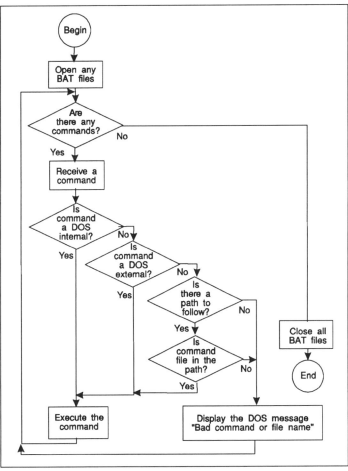

Figure 1-4/3—DOS Command Processor stages

DOS external commands are those which are left in the DOS files on either the DOS diskette or your hard disk. When a DOS internal command is received, it is pulled from the transient section and executed. When a DOS external command is received, such as DISKCOPY, it is taken from the DISCOPY.EXE file providing that file is in root or its location is defined in a path statement. Failure by DOS to find the file results in the message, "Bad command or file name." Figure 1-4/3 tracks the stages following a DOS command.

A path statement is merely an instruction to DOS to look in the directories specified in the path for the file containing the command that has been issued. However, for it to be effective, the path statement must conform to precise rules of structure; as must any entry in the AUTOEXEC.BAT or CONFIG.SYS files.

When DOS receives non-DOS external commands, usually application program files with the EXE or COM extension, it runs them in the resident section of the command processor where, of course, they demand memory. This is the reason why application programs with large command files may not run in a computer with inadequate RAM.

BEYOND THE BASICS

DISK STRUCTURE   Essentially, DOS treats both floppy and hard disks in the same manner, and the following are definitions of DOS disk structure terminology with some disk hardware terminology included for your convenience. Figure 1-4/4 that follows the definitions illustrates disk structure.

- Platter (or disk)—A magnetically coated metal disk, thin and flexible in a floppy disk, rigid and usually stacked one above the other in a hard disk.
- Read/write head—The device that moves across the surface of a disk to write information to the disk or to read information from the disk. The head does not touch the disk. Most disks are double-sided; thus there are two disk drive read/write heads for each disk.
- Tracks—Concentric circles on a disk, not spiral as on a phonograph disk, that are numbered from the outside starting

at 0. Most floppy disks have either 40 or 80 tracks per side, while hard disks have many more, some as many as 1,000.

- Cylinders—Tracks of the same DOS number on each head form a cylinder.
- DOS Sectors—A sector is that part of a track lying within what could be termed "a pie slice" of the disk. If a disk has nine sectors per track and 40 tracks, then there would be 360 sectors.
- Storage capacity—Basically dependent on the number of platters, sides, tracks, and sectors. The regular 5.25" floppy disk stores 512K on each sector, thus the total storage capacity is 2 (sides) x 40 (tracks per side) x 9 (sectors per track) x 512 (bytes) = 368,640 bytes—usually referred to as a 360K disk.
- Clusters—A cluster is a set of contiguous sectors. A 360k floppy has two sectors per cluster, while a hard disk may have 4 or more. DOS allocates disk space by using clusters in an attempt to minimize disk fragmentation.

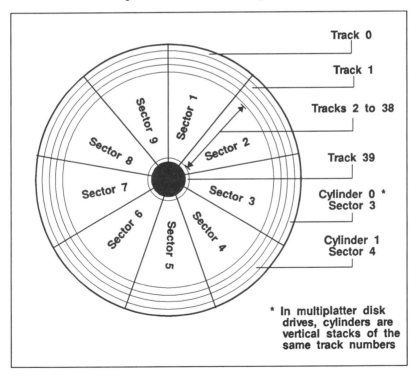

Figure 1-4/4—Disk structure

- Disk fragmentation—Generally caused by frequent editing and deletion of files. If a file is enlarged by editing, and if the contiguous cluster next to it has been used, DOS must place the added data in another cluster, either in an unused area of the disk or in the space created by a deleted file. Fragmentation slows down retrieval time because DOS must read from several parts of the disk, one at a time. Figure 1-4/5 illustrates fragmentation and defragmentation.

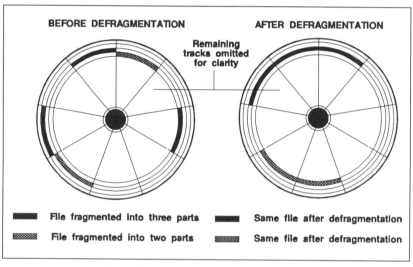

Figure 1-4/5—Simplified illustration of disk defragmentation

- Directory entry—The DOS number of the first cluster in a file and an indicator for the File Allocation Table (FAT).
- FAT—This table contains an entry for each cluster, whether used, available, or corrupted, and is used by DOS for allocating file space and for locating existing files for retrieval.

SOME DOS PROBLEM SOLVING COMMANDS

- ATTRIB—Allows you to set a file's attributes so that it cannot be edited or deleted.
- CHKDSK—Displays the current status of a disk and also displays details of any lost clusters. Clusters can become lost

if while you are working on a file the computer is switched off, either accidentally, by power failure, or after a lock-up.

- COMMAND—Invokes a new command processor in the event the transient portion of the command processor is overwritten by an application program. Typing EXIT allows you to exit from the second command processor.

- LABEL—This command allows you to create a volume label (name) for a disk; useful for disk identification. Some versions of DOS will not allow a disk to be formatted without you first supplying DOS with the volume name.

- MEM /DEBUG|MORE—The MEM command with the DEBUG qualifier types to screen an analysis of your memory address allocations. The |MORE qualifier causes the information to be typed one page at a time.

- RECOVER—While intended to allow you to recover the contents of a corrupted file, minus the bad sectors, this command is considered by many DOS experts to be risky to use.

- SYS—Places the hidden files, IO.SYS and MSDOS.SYS, on to a disk so that the disk becomes bootable.

- VER—Displays the current version of DOS. Some of the newer application programs will not run on older versions of DOS, or will cause operating problems. You use this command to compare your version of DOS with that required by the software.

- VOL—Displays the volume label, if any.

PART TWO
BASIC SYSTEM
TROUBLESHOOTING
AND REPAIRS

Section 2-1

PREVIEW

GROUND RULES

In the event of a problem occuring, observe the simple rules that follow before taking any serious action.

- Keep calm.
- If excessive noise or smoke is emitting from your computer, switch it off regardless of possible loss of data.
- If the problem arises following switching on your computer, make an accurate note of any error messages that are displayed, beeps that your computer emits, or other symptoms, and then power down (switch off).
- If the problem arises during operation, unless your computer actually locks up, endeavor to save what you have been working on, note any system messages, then power down. In either case, after switching off following a lock-up or powering down normally, wait for at least 30 seconds for electrical charges to drain from electronic components within the computer, then try to reboot. This often clears problems that have arisen as a result of simple causes such as fluctuating power supply.
- Always be suspicious of fluctuating power, either from the wall outlet or the transformed output of the power supply that goes to other PC components.

PROPRIETARY DIAGNOSTIC & DISK UTILITY PROGRAMS

There are many diagnostic and/or disk utility programs on the market, some good, some not so good, and selection is very much a matter of individual taste. The most desirable features of a disk utility program are data recovery, disk repair, and disk compression (defragmentation). DOS 5.0 offers some of these features, and DOS 6.0 offers more. The lists that follow are not necessarily comprehensive, but they will give you an indication of what is available together with list prices at the time this book was written. A current edition of a computer magazine such as the *Computer Shopper* might be a better guide. One of the most comprehensive utility programs is PC Tools. The book *Learn PC Tools 8.0 in a Day* is one of the Wordware Publishing, Inc., Popular Applications series and should be available from any good bookstore.

DIAGNOSTIC PROGRAMS

Name	Vendor	List ($)
Checkit	TouchStone Software Corp.	149.00
Infospotter	Merrill & Bryan	79.95
QAPlus	Diagsoft	159.95

DISK UTILITY PROGRAMS

Name	Vendor	List ($)
Norton Utils	Symantec International	179.00
Mace Utils	Fifth Generation Systems	149.00
OPTune	Gazelle Systems, Inc.	99.95
PC Tools	Central Point Software, Inc.	179.00
Spinrite II	Gibson Research Corp.	89.00

Most times you do not need a diagnostic program to tell you that there is a hardware fault; you usually know because something does not work, although there may be occasions when you know that something is wrong but you are not sure exactly what it is. Using Checkit as an example, you are offered a menu choice to test everything, and although this might take a few minutes you will learn what is wrong. However, diagnosing the cause of the problem may not be so simple, especially if the cause is low memory or "dirty" line current. Nevertheless, in the absence of advanced electronic testing gear, a conservatively priced diagnostic program may prove to be a worthwhile investment. Figure 2-1/1 is an example of the items Checkit tests when asked to diagnose a possible serial port fault.

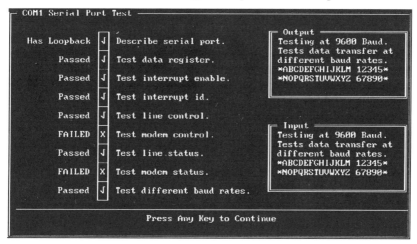

Figure 2-1/1—Serial port test by Checkit

Generally, a disk utility program offering data recovery and disk compression is of more value to you than a diagnostic program, and in any event a good disk utility program may also include limited diagnostic capabilities. PC Tools provides excellent data recovery tools and, if used regularly, its disk compression utility is a valuable tool to help forestall the onset of problems. Figure 2-1/2 shows the PC Tools Compress program window.

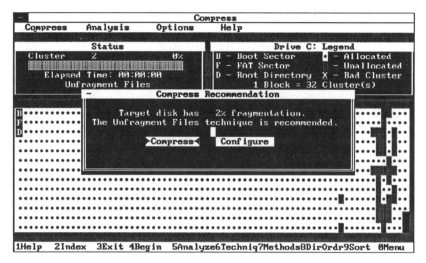

Figure 2-1/2—PC Tools Compress program window

With the competition that exists in the marketplace, software companies vie with each other by regularly introducing upgrades with ever increasing capabilities, often overlapping with other types of programs. For example, word processors have now spread into the desktop publishing realm, and in the same way utility programs have gone beyond plain diagnosis and data recovery by offering features such as communications programs, text editors, and even databases. Study your needs carefully, having in mind the software you already own and your likely future requirements, and in this way you may be able to either select a program that will fulfill more needs than plain diagnostics and data recovery, or avoid duplicating your existing software.

WINDOWS 3.1 MICROSOFT DIAGNOSTIC UTILITY

If you run Microsoft Windows 3.1 and if you have carefully studied the user manual, you will be aware of this useful diagnostic program. It is accessed by typing **MSD <Enter>** at the C:>\WINDOWS prompt. The main menu is shown at Figure 2-1/3.

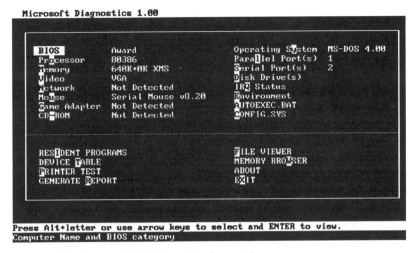

Figure 2-1/3—Microsoft Windows 3.1 diagnostics program

You simply follow the instructions in the message bar at the bottom of the screen to use the utility. A sample menu item is shown at Figure 2-1/4.

```
Microsoft Diagnostics 1.00
┌─ BIOS Information ──────────────────────────────────────────┐
│                                                              │
│        Computer Name: Award                                  │
│        BIOS Category: Original 8 MHz IBM PC/AT or Compatible │
│       Computer Model: FCH    Submodel: 01H                   │
│        BIOS Revision: 00H                                    │
│           BIOS Date: 08/21/91                                │
│                                                              │
│                    DMA Controller Present: Yes               │
│            Fixed disk uses DMA channel 3: No                 │
│        Uses cascaded interrupt 2 (IRQ2): Yes                 │
│                   Real time clock present: Yes               │
│     BIOS keyboard intercept implemented: Yes                 │
│         Wait for external event supported: No                │
│              Extended BIOS data segment: None                │
│              Micro Channel bus present: No                   │
│                                                              │
└──────────────────────────────────────────────────────────────┘
ESC to Cancel or ENTER to Browse BIOS memory area
Computer Name and BIOS category
```

Figure 2-1/4—Example of Microsoft Windows 3.1 diagnostics

67

NONPROPRIETARY DIAGNOSTIC PROGRAMS

There are two types of nonproprietary software: public domain and shareware. Public domain software is exactly as described: software that you may copy, give away, and even sell, with no restrictions placed on you by author's copyrights. Shareware is software that you may copy for the purpose of trying it, but if you decide to use it you must seek approval of the copyright holder, usually for a small fee which also entitles you to updates and manuals.

A few years ago there was no shareware, only public domain software written by amateur programmers anxious to get their name better known. With the advent of the shareware principle, and its organization by its founders, public domain software is becoming history and such utilities that can still be found are few and far between and often not of great value.

Both types of software are sold by vendors such as those found in Appendix C and others whose advertisements you may find in computer magazines. Computer shows or fairs are another source for such software, particularly the smaller, traveling ones that go from town to town and advertise in the local press. Programs other than diagnostic and recovery are also available from such vendors.

The source diskette provided with this book contains a public domain program called Info+ that you use with step-by-step instructions. It is one of the better public domain programs that list the status of the various features of your computer as shown in Figure 2-1/5.

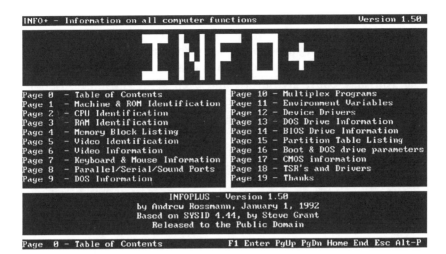

Figure 2-1/5—Info+ main menu

You move about in the program by using the message bar shown at the bottom of the Page 0 screen shown at the foregoing Figure 2-1/4. The procedures follow.

- F1 is the help key which opens a comprehensive help program.

- <Enter> changes "Page 0 - Table of Contents" to "Go to page no >". You then type the page number you want followed by <Enter> to go to that page. Esc used before typing a page number displays the original message.

- PgUp and PgDn moves the screen up or down one program page.

- Home returns you to page 0 and End to page 19.

- Esc returns you to DOS except as previously described.

- Alt-P prints the displayed page to either a file or a printer, which you are able to select.

To use the program perform the following steps.

1. Place the source diskette that came with this book into an appropriate floppy disk drive and type **INFOPLUS <Enter>**.

2. **<Enter>** and then type the page you wish to go to—**16** for this activity, then **<Enter>** again.

69

3. A screen similar to the one shown at Figure 2-1/6 will then display. Observe the information, checking for irregularities that will point to a fault.

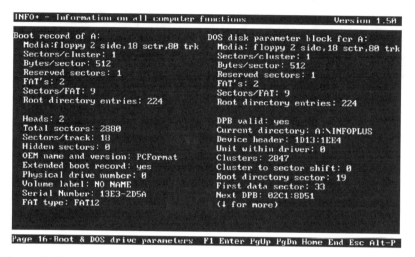

```
INFO+ - Information on all computer functions                    Version 1.50
Boot record of A:                        DOS disk parameter block for A:
  Media:floppy 2 side,18 sctr,80 trk       Media: floppy 2 side,18 sctr,80 trk
  Sectors/cluster: 1                       Sectors/cluster: 1
  Bytes/sector: 512                        Bytes/sector: 512
  Reserved sectors: 1                      Reserved sectors: 1
  FAT's: 2                                 FAT's: 2
  Sectors/FAT: 9                           Sectors/FAT: 9
  Root directory entries: 224              Root directory entries: 224

  Heads: 2                                 DPB valid: yes
  Total sectors: 2880                      Current directory: A:\INFOPLUS
  Sectors/track: 18                        Device header: 1D13:1EE4
  Hidden sectors: 0                        Unit within driver: 0
  OEM name and version: PCFormat           Clusters: 2847
  Extended boot record: yes                Cluster to sector shift: 0
  Physical drive number: 0                 Root directory sector: 19
  Volume label: NO NAME                    First data sector: 33
  Serial Number: 13E3-2D5A                 Next DPB: 02C1:8D51
  FAT type: FAT12                          (↓ for more)

Page 16-Boot & DOS drive parameters   F1 Enter PgUp PgDn Home End Esc Alt-P
```

Figure 2-1/6—Info+ boot record program

4. Select the other pages of the menu in turn, and observe the information displayed.

5. Press **Esc** to return to DOS.

Section 2-2

SOME STARTUP PROBLEMS AND IMMEDIATE RESPONSES

SYMPTOMS

Like a human, your PC will display a symptom if it is sick, and although it cannot explain its problems with quite the same clarity as a human, it can talk to you and does so either by beep-codes via the speaker or by screen messages. Unfortunately, few models display the same messages or use the same beep-code, but by referring to your system user manual, you can establish what your computer does when it's in trouble. Under normal conditions, with any model, you may expect to hear from the speaker the memory count and then a single short beep as DOS takes over. If you hear more than that, you know you have a problem of some sort. The beep-code messages transmitted by some makes of BIOS consist of long beeps only, whereas the Phoenix BIOS, as an example, uses a more advanced code with both long and short beeps which, in different combinations (the binary system), are able to convey many more fault conditions. If your computer communicates with you by screen message, get into the habit of checking the results of the diagnostic checks each time you start your machine; it is so easy to ignore these checks and, if trouble occurs, you can waste hours attempting to find a problem your PC has already displayed during the diagnostic check.

Beep codes usually cover the failures shown in the list that follows.

- DRAM refresh failure
- Parity circuitry failure
- First 64KB base memory failure
- System timer failure
- Processor failure
- Keyboard controller failure
- Virtual mode exception error
- Display memory read/write test failure
- ROM BIOS checksum error

Screen messages also vary with the make of ROM BIOS but the message is always understandable. For example, one make of ROM BIOS might report "No keyboard," while another make displays "Keyboard bad," but in either case you know you have a keyboard problem. Again, different makes of ROM BIOS display different messages during power-up; some do little more than display their name and count the memory, while others display comprehensive diagnostic checks, and Figure 2-2/1 is an example of the latter.

```
386SX-SUPERCHECK-03 Modular BIOS Version 3.01
Copyright 1990-92 Super Software Inc.
386SX Version 3.2P

TESTING INTERRUPT CONTROLLER #1. . . . . . . . . . . . . .PASS
TESTING INTERRUPT CONTROLLER #2. . . . . . . . . . . . . .PASS
TESTING CMOS BATTERY. . . . . . . . . . . . . . . . . . . . . .PASS
TESTING CMOS CHECKSUM . . . . . . . . . . . . . . . . . . . .PASS
SIZING SYSTEM MEMORY. . . . . . . . . . . . . . . . .640K FOUND
TESTING SYSTEM MEMORY. . . . . . . . . . . . . . . .640K PASS
CHECKING UNEXPECTED INTERRUPTS AND STUCK NMI. . .PASS
TESTING PROTECTED MODE. . . . . . . . . . . . . . . . . . .PASS
SIZING EXTENDED MEMORY. . . . . . . . . . . . .01024K FOUND
TESTING MEMORY IN PROTECTED MODE. . . . . . .01664K PASS
TESTING PROCESSOR EXCEPTION INTERRUPTS. . . . . . .PASS
BIOS SHADOW RAM. . . . . . . . . . . . . . . . . . . . . .ENABLED
VIDEO SHADOW RAM . . . . . . . . . . . . . . . . . . . . .ENABLED

<PRESS CTRL+ALT+ESC FOR SETUP>
```

Figure 2-2/1—BIOS diagnostic checks

If a fault is displayed, your action should be to power down and proceed to the next sections where you will find out how to rectify the problem.

Symptoms indicating faults fall into the two categories of hardware and software, and in this section we will deal with them in that order. Following each listed symptom, immediate response actions are given, but if the steps you take do not correct the fault, you must proceed to the next sections which deal in greater depth with problems and remedies.

HARDWARE

The list that follows details the startup hardware symptoms that might occur and the immediate, basic responses you can take.

Problem After switching on, no activity from computer, monitor, keyboard, or any other peripheral.

Response Check line supply from electrical wall outlet; check line supply from voltage regulator or surge suppresser if present; check computer power cable for proper connection at each end.

Problem After switching on you have no video, no keyboard LED lights, and the computer emits a series of beeps.

Response Record the number of beeps, power down, check the beep-codes in your user manual to identify the fault, and then proceed to the next sections to determine the action you should take.

Problem After switching on, computer appears to boot (or emits a series of beeps), keyboard LEDs function, but there is no video.

Response Confirm that the monitor ON/OFF switch is on; check adjustment of brightness control; check line supply from electrical wall outlet, the voltage regulator/surge suppresser, or from second power supply socket at the back of the computer. Check video cable connections at each end.

Problem Screen message indicates keyboard fault.

Response Confirm that keyboard cable is properly connected to computer. If it is a switching keyboard, check that the XT/AT switch on the underside of the keyboard is correctly selected.

SOFTWARE

Unless you are connected to a network, the only software problems you are likely to encounter until you load an application program will be those associated with the startup and boot procedures.

If you believe your problem is network related, refer it to your network supervisor—that is what they are for. In the case of problems with application programs, because of the many and diverse programs in use, it is virtually impossible to come up with a set of procedures that will solve problems that arise with them. Often, the program user manual will have a trouble-shooting section, and that may help. Next, of course, is to make use of whatever support facilities are offered by the software company, which is a better bet than calling for help from your local computer company representative, who may not be very familiar with the particular program, even if he or she sold it to you in the first place. Salespeople, technicians, and support personnel from computer stores tend, by necessity, to be "Jacks or Jills of all trades, but masters of none."

Possible problems and immediate responses associated with startup and boot procedures are shown in the list that follows.

Problem   On ATs, screen announcement telling you that the configuration is incorrect.

Response   Enter setup and change whichever item is incorrect. A typical setup program is shown at Figure 2-2/2.

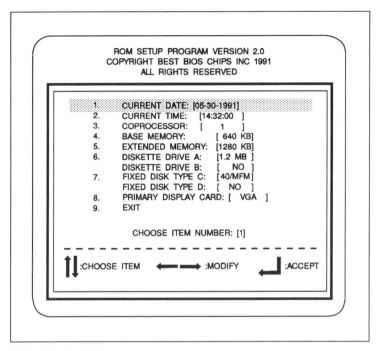

Figure 2-2/2—Typical setup screen

Problem Screen displays the message, "Disk boot failure, insert system disk and press Enter" (or one similar to it).

Response If you are booting from a floppy diskette, insert a bootable diskette into drive A; if you are booting from a hard disk, attempt a reboot, but if this fails, boot from a diskette and attempt to access the hard disk. If you can access it, try transferring the system files to it and then reboot. If you cannot access the hard disk after booting from a diskette, or if the previous solution fails, power down and refer to the next sections.

Problem Screen displays the message, "Non-system disk or disk error. Replace and strike any key when ready."

Response If you are booting from a diskette, remove the nonboot diskette from drive A and replace with a bootable diskette. If you are booting from a hard disk, follow the procedures given in the previous Problem and Response in this list.

75

Problem Screen message, "Bad or missing Command Interpreter."

Response If you are booting from a diskette, try a different diskette. If you are booting from a hard disk, reboot using a bootable diskette, then transfer the file COMMAND.COM to the root directory on your hard disk. If you are using a COMMSPEC= entry, be sure that the environment parameter points to a valid directory containing the COMMAND.COM file. To transfer the COMMAND.COM file, from root use the DOS COPY command to copy the file from whichever directory it is in, usually a DOS directory. For example, C:\>COPY C:\DOS\COMMAND.COM <Enter>.

Problem Screen message, "Bad or missing <filename>."

Response Check the CONFIG.SYS file to ensure it contains appropriate device driver file name and that it is correctly entered.

Problem Screen message, "Cannot load COMMAND, system halted."

Response Reboot DOS.

Problem Screen message, "Cannot start COMMAND, exiting."

Response Because this problem is likely to be caused by DOS finding insufficient memory to invoke a copy of the command processor owing to too many device drivers or other memory users, remove one or more nonessential device drivers and reboot. To temporarily remove a device driver, either follow any instructions provided with the device's user manual, or use EDLIN or a text editor to simply place an asterisk at the beginning of the DEVICE= line in the AUTOEXEC.BAT file. To later reinstate the device, remove the asterisk using EDLIN or a text editor and then reboot.

Problem Screen message, "Error loading operating system."

Response Reboot DOS from drive A, transfer the system files to the hard disk, and then reboot from the hard disk. To transfer the system files after booting from a diskette, type SYS C: <Enter>.

Problem   Screen message, "Missing operating system."

Response   Because the DOS startup procedures are unable to continue as a result of a bootable DOS partition not containing DOS, you must boot from a floppy, back up your hard disk, and then reformat the DOS partition with the FORMAT/S command. Section 2-11 covers formatting in detail.

Problem   Screen message, "Top level process aborted, cannot continue."

Response   Reboot with a different DOS diskette.

Section 2-3

DATA AND DISK RECOVERY

INTRODUCTION

Whereas data and disk recovery may not be truly classified as repairs, they surely count as repairs if you have lost data as a result of inadvertent erasure, inadvertent formatting, or corrupted disks, and you are able to recover the data. Among the various problems that can occur in computing, loss of data is probably the most common.

Files may be undeleted and disks unformatted or repaired with software such as DOS 5.0, PC Tools, Norton Utilities, Mace, etc. For undeleting files, DOS 5.0 uses an efficient utility provided by the manufacturers of PC Tools; however, the DOS RECOVER command, used to repair damaged disks, takes second place next to similar tools in other proprietary utility programs. From a utility point of view, DOS 6.0 is a marked improvement. PC Tools 8.0 is an excellent program for data and disk and the book, *Learn PC Tools 8.0 in a Day*, is available from Wordware Publishing. Lost data may also be recovered by sending the disk containing the data to commercial companies that specialize in this activity.

Notwithstanding the foregoing, the finest way to protect data is by backing up. You should back up as often as is feasible, preferably automatically each night using a tape backup system. If regular backups are not possible, always make a copy to a diskette of important new files or edits. For this purpose it pays to set up a simple diskette filing system so that you can keep track of copies, and so that you can delete the files following your next full backup.

DISK PROTECTION

Preventative maintenance and preparation for possible loss—disk protection—is more important than any other aspect of data recovery. DOS and proprietary utility programs provide the means to protect your disks by using specific utilities.

DOS The utilities available differ with different versions of DOS. If the version you are using does not have all the utilities, use a proprietary program if you have one, or consider upgrading your DOS. Upgrading to DOS 5.0 or 6.0 will give you many advantages over and above data and disk recovery features.

The ATTRIB Command (Available in most versions of DOS) With this command you change the attributes of a file to make it "read only," thereby avoiding the possibility of accidental deletion or editing by an unauthorized person. To make a file read only, you type the ATTRIB command followed by + and the filename. To remove the read only restriction you type the same string but change + to -. You can use DOS wildcards to change groups of files; for example, ATTRIB + *.SYS <Enter> would change all your system files in the active directory to read only. ATTRIB + *.* <Enter> would change all the files in the directory to read only.

The MIRROR Command (Not available in versions prior to 5.0) This command saves information about a disk to a special file, thereby enhancing any subsequent recovery action. You can type the command at the DOS prompt to apply it to floppy diskettes or hard disk drives. However, the logical place for it is on a hard disk drive in the AUTOEXEC.BAT file so that a mirror image is made each time you boot your PC. If you add a /T switch, DOS will also keep specific track of deleted files, but you must also specify the directory and, if you wish, the maximum number of files to be tracked preceded by a - sign. Table 2-3/1 gives the default number of deleted files that will be stored according to disk size in a DOS PCTRACKR.DEL file.

Disk Size	Number of entries	Size of PCTRACKR.DEL file
360K	25	5K
720K	50	9K
1.2MB	75	14K
1.44MB	75	14K
20MB	101	18K
32MB	202	36K
Over 32MB	303	55K

Table 2-3/1—Default number of stored deleted files

Typical mirror commands would be MIRROR /TA-50 or MIRROR /TC-500.

PROPRIETARY PROGRAMS PC Tools is one of several programs that offer disk protection utilities. The PC Tools utilities are Write Protection, Data Monitor, and Mirror.

Write Protection A tool that prevents protected data from deletion, damage, and being overwritten. It can be loaded into memory each time you use your computer and, from a simple menu, you specify the area of your disk to be protected as shown in the following list.

- Entire disk—Prevents the entire disk from being written to.
- System areas—Protects those areas of your disk such as the boot sector and the FAT (File Allocation Table).
- Listed files—Prevents specified files from being written to.

Data Monitor A memory-resident program with the Delete Protection part designed to protect your computer against data loss. Delete Protection provides two protective methods that help increase your chances of recovering lost data: Delete Sentry and Delete Tracker.

Delete Sentry—Automatically saves deleted files in a hidden directory called SENTRY, making recovery certain.

Delete Tracker—Saves from the files information that will help recovery but not guarantee it.

You specify the percentage of your hard drive that you are willing to allocate to the hidden SENTRY directory and the number of days after which you want deleted files automatically purged from that directory.

Mirror A program that saves a copy of the information in the system area of your hard disk in order to enhance unformat and disk recovery procedures.

UNDELETING

When you delete a file using the DOS DELETE command, intentionally or inadvertently, DOS removes the file name from the directory, writes a hex code over the first character, and then leaves the data on the disk until the space is taken by another file, i.e., written over. DOS also removes the FAT entries for the file in order to free up space. DOS 5.0 and proprietary utility software programs provide undelete utilities that help you recover accidentally deleted files and directories that have not been written over. It is most effective when your files are protected by the data protection methods already described. Both the DOS 5.0 UNDELETE command and PC Tools Undelete will ask you to supply the first character of the deleted file, and they then set about restoring the FAT entries. Figure 2-3/1 shows a list of deleted files ready for undeleting by DOS 5.0.

```
 Deletion-tracking file not found.

 MS-DOS directory contains    13 deleted files.
 Of those,    13 files may be recovered.

Using the MS-DOS directory.

      ?UTOEXEC BAT       10  4-09-91  5:00a  ...A
      ?OMMAND  COM    47845  4-09-91  5:00a  ...A
      ?ETUP    INI    11399  4-09-91  5:00a  ...A
      ?NINSTAL EXE    89220  4-09-91  5:00a  ...A
      ?IOS     OLD    33430  4-09-91  5:00a  ...A
      ?OS      OLD    37394  4-09-91  5:00a  ...A
      ?OMMAND  DAT    47845  4-09-91  5:00a  ...A
      ?BOOT0   DAT      512  1-07-93  9:21a  ...A
      ?BOOT    DAT      512  1-07-93  9:21a  ...A
      ?PB0     DAT       86  1-07-93  9:21a  ...A
      ?LOBAL   DAT      703  1-07-93  9:21a  ...A
      ?OOT     DAT    16384  1-07-93  9:21a  ...A
      ?AT      DAT    62464  1-07-93  9:21a  ...A


Press any key to return to MS-DOS Shell....
```

Figure 2-3/1—DOS 5.0 undelete utility

With most undelete programs you can accomplish the tasks in the list that follows.

- Undelete files automatically
- Undelete files manually
- Undelete files on a network
- Undelete directories
- Browse directories to select from a list of deleted files
- Find deleted files by specification
- View files before undeleting them
- Scan a disk for lost deleted files and portions of files

Notwithstanding the apparent efficiency of undelete programs, if the space occupied by the deleted file gets written over, there is no chance of recovery. If disk fragmentation "splits" up the deleted file, an undelete program is usually not able to undelete automatically and you are asked to undelete manually—not always an easy task.

UNFORMATTING

In the event you accidentally format a disk, there are available utilities such as DOS 5.0 and PC Tools to assist in recovery, but full recovery of your data will depend on how the disk was formatted, how soon after accidental formatting you attempt unformatting, and whether or not Mirror was used. You should use unformat utilities only to attempt recovery from a disastrous mistake. The techniques used, common to most unformat utilities, are explained in the paragraphs that follow.

HARD DISKS   Disks formatted with the DOS 5.0 or later FORMAT command using the /U switch cannot be recovered. With disks that were formatted without the /U switch, or by earlier versions of DOS, unformat utilities rebuild the File Allocation Table and the directory structure (root directory, subdirectories, and files) either from the file created by mirror programs, or from hard disk data.

FLOPPY DISKETTES   Recovery is not normally possible because DOS FORMAT.COM permanently erases data from a floppy diskette. However, if the diskette was formatted with PC Tool's PC Format, recovery is possible.

DISK REPAIR

Most of the proprietary disk recovery software programs include a disk repair feature not available in the DOS utilities.

If a disk becomes corrupted, you can attempt to recover the files with DOS by using the RECOVER command. (With DOS 6.0, the RECOVER command has been retired.) However, not only is this utility unable to recover the parts of the files on the corrupted areas of the disk, but the utility itself is generally not recommended by experienced users. In any event, the utility is unable to actually repair the disk except by reformatting after, hopefully, you have recovered as much data as possible. Recovered data is written to root in files beginning with FILE0001.REC. With DOS 6.0, the RECOVER command has been retired. Alternatively, utilities such as the PC Tools DiskFix can be almost 100% effective, particularly if used in conjunction with Mirror. Furthermore, a program such as DiskFix can usually be used in a preventative capacity to avoid potential disk problems. The utility's main menu is shown at Figure 2-3/2.

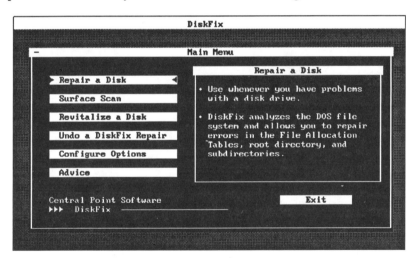

Figure 2-3/2—PC Tools DiskFix main menu

The DiskFix utility is able to carry out the following functions.

REPAIR MOST DISK PROBLEMS Repair disks that have become corrupted with damage to partition tables and boot sectors, and correct errors such as cross-linked files and lost cluster chains.

RECOVER "LOST" DATA   Bring back both files and directories contained in lost clusters.

PROTECT DATA FROM MEDIA DEFECTS   Find and repair damaged data, moving the data to a safe location if necessary.

REMOVE MEDIA DEFECTS FROM USE   Locate and anticipate media surface defects and remove them from use.

PERFORM A NONDESTRUCTIVE LOW-LEVEL FORMAT When DOS is having trouble reading or writing data, the disk can be revitalized without damage to data.

OPTIMIZE HARD DISK PERFORMANCE   Set the hard disk interleave for optimum performance without destroying data.

FIND VIRUSES   Detect hidden viruses in any system area.

When you use the program it checks for faults and shows the percentage completed for each test performed. These tests are given in the list that follows.

- Boot Sector
- FAT Integrity
- FAT Comparison
- FAT Data Analysis
- Directory Structure
- Media Descriptors
- Lost Clusters
- Cross-linked Files

The program checks and OKs passed tests. If a fault is found, you will be given the opportunity to make a copy of the affected data before an attempt is made to correct it. When the fault has been corrected, the test will be marked FIXED.

TIP When you are using the utility to fix a problem on your hard drive, it is wise to make a copy of affected data when given the opportunity. By doing so, you will later be able to restore your disk to its original state should repair not be possible. You would carry out this restore by choosing PC Tool's Undo a DiskFix Repair. If a fault is found that cannot be corrected, a recommendation is made to attempt fault correction by revitalizing the disk.

When lost clusters are found, you are given the option of deleting them (if you know you do not need the data that might be in them) or recovering the files/directories lost in the clusters and writing them to the root directory as PCTnnnnn.FIX for files, or LOSTnnnn.SUB for directories. You can then examine and rename the *.FIX and *.SUB files. Any files contained in recovered directories will have their original names and will be intact.

DISK RECOVERY SERVICES

Various computer magazines carry advertisements placed by companies who claim to specialize in data recovery from damaged or corrupted disks, but the author is unable to find sufficient evidence to recommend using a particular company that offers this type of service. However, the National Computer Security Association, 4401-A Connecticut Avenue N.W., Suite 309, Washington, DC 20015, Tel: (202) 364-8252 should be able to offer advice. If you have important data on a corrupted disk, and you are unable to recover the data by using disk utility software such as PC Tools, before sending it to a data recovery company attempt to make a backup, or copies, of any files that are accessible.

Section 2-4

DISASSEMBLY INSTRUCTIONS

NOTE

Bear in mind that while the component removal and installation procedures detailed in the various sections of this book apply to most makes of IBM-compatible PCs, there is always the "odd man out" and, if you have it, you must adapt the steps to suit.

WORK SPACE

A desk or table of at least four feet by two feet is acceptable, but five by three is better. If you can cover the work area with a cloth that you don't mind getting soiled, not only will you avoid scratching the surface of the desk or table, but the surface will be less slippery and dropped screws will be more likely to stay put instead of skittering off into a dark corner of the room.

Try to give yourself comfortable access to all sides of the work surface because you will find you will want to view your PC from various angles. However, while you are moving around, take care not to get caught up with any cables. Dragging your PC or monitor off the work surface and onto the floor could cause even greater problems.

PREPARATION

Careful preparation will pay great dividends at any time, but even more so if you are opening up your PC for the first time. Begin by removing from the area where you plan to work all unnecessary items such as books, paper, pencils, diskettes, etc.

Next, provide yourself with half-a-dozen small containers for storing screws and other small parts (cups will do if you have nothing else), and a couple of cardboard boxes for holding larger parts (shoe boxes or the type of boxes stationary and envelopes are supplied in will do fine).

Make sure you have a good light source and, in addition, make available a small flashlight with good batteries.

Be sure you have use of the planned work area for adequate time. Once you have your PC broken down into component parts, there is nothing worse than having to pack it all together in order to move elsewhere—almost a guarantee of more trouble.

If you suspect your problem is a faulty monitor, keyboard, floppy disk drive, or similar major item, endeavor to borrow a replacement from a friend or associate to use to check out your suspicions. If your monitor does not work on your PC, but another monitor does, then you do not need to look any further for the problem. However, if a known serviceable monitor does not function on your PC, then the cable or video card becomes suspect. If you do use a borrowed peripheral or component for testing purpose, make sure it has the same specifications as the one you suspect is faulty.

TOOLS

The first three tools in the following list are essential for disassembly and reassembly. The others in the list are desirable but you can get by without them.

    No. 2 Phillips screwdriver
    3/16" flat blade screwdriver
    Pointed nose pliers

    Memory extractor and inserter
    Tweezers

Magnifying glass
Flashlight
Small containers for loose screws etc.
Magnet (useful to magnetize screwdrivers in order to prevent screws from falling into your computer case where they could short out circuits, but keep all magnets and magnetized objects well away from floppy and hard disks)

DISASSEMBLY

CAUTION

Before working on your PC at any time, discharge the static electricity from your body by touching a grounded metal object. If you feel comfortable leaving the power cable connected to your PC, touching the chassis makes an excellent ground. In a very dry environment, wear a grounding wrist strap.

PRELIMINARY   Perform the steps that follow to prepare your PC for disassembly.

1. Disconnect the power cable at the back of your PC if you need to remove the power supply, but consider leaving it connected as a means for grounding static electricity if you plan to work only on other components.

2. Disconnect the keyboard cable from your PC and place the keyboard in a safe place.

3. Disconnect the video cable from the back of your PC along with any other cables such as those for a mouse, a scanner, a network, etc.

TIP If you are in an office environment and your PC is connected to a network, have your network system supervisor assist in the disconnect. If you are not on a network and you are unfamiliar with any connected cables, or believe you might forget which is which, label each cable and affix another label to the back of your PC in the appropriate position.

4. Disconnect the power cable from your monitor, or from the source of power supply, then locate the monitor in a safe place.

REMOVING THE COVER There are two basic designs of PC cases: desktop and tower, and each have further subdesign features. The cover of a desktop model may be secured by screws at the back of the PC, or at the sides, and Figure 2-4/1 illustrates these two methods.

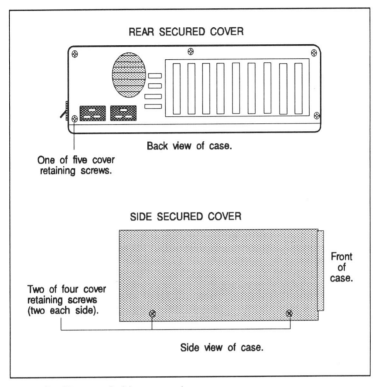

Figure 2-4/1—Rear and side secured covers

Tower cases may be full-size or mini, but most times the cover securing screws are at the rear of the case.

If you have a user manual for your PC, regardless of the type of case check it for cover removal instructions and follow them. If instructions are not provided or if you do not have a manual, perform the steps that follow.

1. Remove the cover securing screws from either the rear or the sides of the case and store them in a container, labeling the container "Cover screws."

2. Remove the cover in one of the following ways:

   a. With most tower or mini-tower cases, withdraw the cover backwards off the PC case, levering at the back with a thin-bladed screwdriver if necessary. However, there are some cases where the front must be removed first.

   b. With a rear secured cover on a desktop case, withdraw the cover forwards off the PC case.

TIP Locating guides in the front inside of a desktop case may prevent the cover from sliding easily. If this is so, place a pad (for protection) against one of the back top corners, then strike it sharply with a closed fist. (This is best achieved by leaning over the front of the case, holding the pad with the left hand, and striking the padded corner with the clenched small finger part of the fist). This action will free the cover from the guides and allow it to slide all the way off.

   c. With a side secured cover on a desktop case, withdraw the cover backwards far enough to free the cover lip from under the front bezel of the PC case, then lift the cover straight up and off.

3. Locate the cover in a safe place.

If your PC is a tower or mini-tower model, carefully lay it flat on the side that leaves all the components visible. In the case of a desktop AT, the inside of your PC should resemble the illustration at Figure 2-4/2 if the memory is DIP, and a tower or mini-tower on its side should be sufficiently similar for you to be able to identify the components.

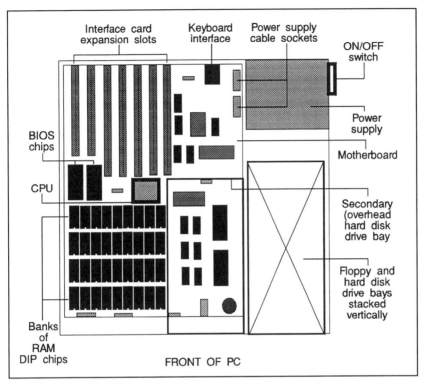

Figure 2-4/2—Under the cover of a desktop AT

More recent motherboards, fitted with SIMM or SIP memory, are likely to be smaller as a result of the memory sockets taking up much less space. Generally, the size reduction is in the front to back plane, with the width being unchanged. When these newer motherboards are installed in one of the older-version cases, there is space to spare near the front of the PC case. However, integrated new models may have a smaller case to suit the motherboard, although with most layouts there is little space to spare between the back of the principal drive bay and the power supply case.

Your PC is now ready for component removal.

Section 2-5

KEYBOARDS

OVERVIEW

Keyboard failures are invariably associated with age or misuse. Misuse involves long exposure to adverse environmental conditions such as dust and smoke, and man-made adverse conditions such as spilled coffee. Pollution of this nature can interfere with the keys making proper contact with their microswitches when pressed, or inhibit the action of the microswitches.

In order to facilitate cleaning, keys can be pried off of most computers using two thin-bladed screwdrivers, one each side of the key. Alternatively, a better tool is a chip puller which you should be able to obtain from your local computer store. If you remove more than one key at a time, make a drawing to assist you in replacing them in the correct place, or have a similar keyboard handy to use as a pattern. Replacing keys in the wrong position can be frustrating. For example, if the A key is inadvertently replaced in the S position, when pressed it will type "S" to the screen and not "A"—something you may not even notice until you commence reading a printout.

Reference was made earlier in this book to XT/AT switchable keyboards, but some expansion of the information that was given may be helpful at this point. An XT keyboard has the keyboard BIOS in the keyboard, while an AT keyboard expects to find the BIOS on the motherboard and, as a result, the two types of keyboard are not interchangeable. In an XT/AT switchable keyboard, the printed circuits from the key/microswitches go to the XT/AT switch, then circuits from the switch go either to an XT-type keyboard BIOS in the keyboard, or to the AT-type keyboard BIOS on the motherboard.

A keyboard cable can be damaged by being continually stretched as a result of your PC being located too far from the keyboard (e.g., under your desk). Keyboard cable extensions are available from most good computer stores.

Beyond simple cleaning there is not too much you can do to repair a faulty keyboard, and replacement is often the most economic course to take, particularly with keyboards being available for as little as $20.

Disconnect your keyboard from the computer before working on it.

PROBLEMS AND RESPONSES

Problem Your PC is running but the keyboard is dead—no LED lights and keys are ineffective.

Response

1. Check the interface with the PC.
2. Check the XT/AT switch if there is one.
3. If your keyboard is very old, repair attempts are unlikely to be successful, and with the relatively low price of off-brand name keyboards you should consider buying a new one. With a new keyboard you will have the full range of function keys (F1 to F12) which you may find useful with some application programs. Section 4-6 assists you in selection.

Problem A key sticks down after it is pressed.

Response

1. With keyboards that have a membrane covering the internal circuits and pressure switches, use high pressure air to blow out the accumulated dirt. Most computer or electronic stores sell aerosol cans of compressed air. If you use liquid to wash out the dirt, choose a pure alcohol or its equivalent, and use it sparingly after pulling the offending key.
2. With keyboards that do not have a membrane covering the internal circuits and pressure switches, air pressure is not advised because it can blow the dirt into other exposed areas of the internal circuit board. Pull the offending key and use a cotton stick-swab dipped in pure alcohol or its equivalent to carefully clean the area under the key.

Problem   A key fails to print its letter to the screen.

Response   Because this problem is only likely to happen with keyboards not fitted with a protective membrane, follow the previous response number 2, ensuring that the pressure switch contact is cleaned.

PREVENTIVE MAINTENANCE

- Use a keyboard cover when your PC is not in use.
- Keep food and drink away from the keyboard.
- Maintain a clean environment (smoke of any sort fouls the environment).
- Periodically use a vacuum cleaner to suck dust from between the keys.
- When cleaning the surfaces of the keys, only use a pure alcohol, or its equivalent, and a soft cloth. Paper tends to shred and leave lint which falls between the keys.

Section 2-6

MONITORS AND VIDEO CARDS

OVERVIEW

Monitors and video cards are not physically repairable except by skilled technicians. If for any reason you open up the back of a monitor, be sure the power cable is disconnected from its power source, and wait for a considerable time before touching any internal part. Monitors have high volume storage capacitors which can cause dangerous electric shocks.

If you determine that either your monitor or video card is beyond your capability to repair, make careful comparisons between the cost of replacement and the cost of professional repair. With computer technician rates running at up to $100.00 and more per hour, repair may not be an option.

PROBLEMS AND RESPONSES

Problem   Your PC is running but the monitor is dead.

Response

1. Check the power connection to the monitor and that the monitor is switched on.
2. Check the interface with the video card.
3. Check the dimmer switch for adequate brightness.

4. With a color monitor, ascertain from the user manual if there is an accessible fuse at the back. Reseating a good fuse that is not making a good contact sometimes solves the problem. If it is faulty, replace it.

5. Check that the application software you are running will recognize your monitor type.

6. With an AT, check that setup is correctly configured for the type of monitor in use.

7. With an XT check that dip switches are properly set for the type of monitor in use.

8. Reseat the video card (pull it and reinstall it) to ensure a satisfactory connection to the bus.

9. Try the monitor on another PC properly configured for your type of monitor. If the monitor functions, the indications are that your video card is faulty.

Problem   Your monitor displays "snow."

Response

1. Check your video card for compatibility with your monitor.

2. Check that the video card dip switch settings and jumper positions are correct for your type of monitor. The video card user manual should provide this information.

Problem   You have either screen distortion, a vertically "rolling" screen, or an incorrectly sized screen.

Response   If accessible, adjust either the vertical or horizontal sync controls. Refer to your monitor user manual for the location of these controls. If they are not accessible, have a trained technician make the adjustment.

Problem   Characters do not display correctly.

Response   Use diagnostic software such as Checkit to ascertain if there is a fault with the video card memory, which is the likely cause of the problem. If it is, replace the memory if it is not soldered, or if it is soldered, replace the card.

REPLACING A MONITOR

1. Power down your PC.
2. Switch off your monitor.
3. Disconnect the monitor power cable.
4. Disconnect the monitor cable from the video card interface at the back of your PC.
5. Check that the jumpers and/or switch settings are correctly set to suit your new monitor on the video card and, for an XT, on the motherboard.
6. Connect the monitor power cable and switch on to ensure that power is reaching the monitor by observing either screen activity or the power indicator light.
7. Interface the monitor video cable to your video card, screwing it tightly into position.
8. Boot your computer and, with an AT, if the monitor specifications differ from the old one, enter setup and record the changes.
9. Adjust the brightness controls to your satisfaction.

REPLACING A VIDEO CARD

1. Power down your PC and remove its cover.
2. Disconnect the video cable from the card.
3. Remove the screw that locks the card's end cover to the PC's back plate.
4. Grip the card firmly between fingers and thumb, avoiding sharp wire ends on the back of the card and fragile devices on the front of the card, then remove it using a rocking motion if it does not pull easily.
5. Set any jumpers and/or switches on the new card according to instructions in the card's user manual for your type of monitor.
6. Press the card firmly into an expansion slot on the motherboard, ensuring that the bronze-colored connector is in the right position.

7. Replace the screw to lock the end cover of the card to the back plate of your PC.

8. Interface the video cable to the card, screwing it in tightly.

9. Switch on your monitor and boot your PC.

PREVENTIVE MAINTENANCE

- Switch off your monitor when it is not in use.
- Place a cover over your monitor when it is not in use.
- Consider using a screen saver if you leave your monitor switched on but unattended for long periods of time.

Section 2-7

POWER SUPPLIES

OVERVIEW

Basically, no part of a power supply is repairable and, in any event, you should observe the warning on the case telling you not to open it.

A power supply is more susceptible to failure than any other component of a PC other than, perhaps, a floppy disk drive. It is also absolutely critical to the operation of the computer, and if it is malfunctioning, it can cause extensive and expensive damage to other components. Power supplies are relatively inexpensive and if you suspect yours is faulty, do not hesitate to replace it, but be sure the new specification is correct for your PC.

PROBLEMS AND RESPONSES

Problem   Your PC will not start and you have checked power cable connections.

Response   Confirm if the fan is rotating by checking for a flow of air coming out of the back of the unit or by listening for the noise of the fan motor. If the fan is not working, the odds are that the power supply has failed and you must replace it, and even if by chance only the fan unit has failed, you will still need to replace it because the cost of professional repair of the fan/motor is likely to exceed the cost of a new power supply.

Problem Observable problems such as mysterious lockups or hard disk drive inconsistencies make you suspect a faulty power supply. Under voltage may be the cause of these problems.

Response Have a qualified person check the voltages of your power supply.

Problem Failure of drive motors, memory chips, etc. lead you to suspect you have a faulty power supply. (Over voltage output from the power supply over a lengthy period may put strain on other electronic parts and cause failures.)

Response Have a qualified person check the voltages of your power supply.

POWER SUPPLY REMOVAL

1. Disconnect the 4-pin cables from any installed drives.
2. Disconnect the power supply cables from the motherboard.

TIP Most power supply connectors have a centrally located plastic spring clip on one side of the connector which must be eased away from the socket on the motherboard before you can disconnect.

3. Remove the screws from the back panel of your PC's chassis where they lock the power supply in position. Store them in a safe place.
4. Slide the power supply away from the back of the chassis until the tongue and slot locking device on the bottom of the power supply is released and the unit can be removed.

POWER SUPPLY REPLACEMENT

1. Position the power supply so that you can slide the slot in the unit's base over the raised tongue on the computer chassis.
2. Secure the unit to the back of the computer chassis using the screws removed from the old power supply.

3. Identify the power supply connector with an orange cable at one end. Grip the connector so that the orange cable is nearest the back wall of the computer chassis and so that the connector itself is immediately above the end of the ribbon connector socket nearest the back wall of the computer case. See Figure 1-2/10 in Section 1-2.

4. Tilt the top of the connector away from the power supply and engage the peg on the connector with the small slot in the socket. Straighten the connector while pressing down to complete a secure interface. Repeat the procedure for second connector.

5. Connect 4-pin power cables to installed drives.

PREVENTIVE MAINTENANCE

- Maintain a well-ventilated and clean environment.
- Switch off your PC when not in use.

Section 2-8
MEMORY

OVERVIEW

Memory problems generally relate to faulty chips, although there are other causes such as an inadvertent change in the memory switch settings on an XT, or in the setup program on an AT. The latter can be caused by electrical storms. Under or over voltage from the power supply can also cause memory problems. Whatever the cause, with a memory problem your PC should display an error message or emit a beep code which you can use in conjunction with the user manual to identify the problem.

PROBLEMS AND RESPONSES

Problem   Your AT displays a parity error during the power-up self-diagnosis.

Response

1. Enter the setup program, if necessary correct wrong entries, then exit for reboot.
2. Carry out the checks detailed under Basic Responses later in this section.

Problem   You have an old model PC with the memory chips soldered to the board and you get a memory problem message.

Response   You can remove the motherboard for chip testing and replacement by a qualified service person. However, chip replacement costs may be more than the cost of a replacement motherboard and memory and, in any event, with such an old motherboard you will benefit from an upgrade.

Problem Your PC develops a memory problem during normal operations.

Response Attempt to save your work, then carry out the checks detailed under Basic Responses later in this section, powering down as necessary.

BASIC RESPONSES

You carry out in turn the responses that follow until the cause of the problem is cleared or identified.

1. Check the dip switches on an XT or rerun setup on an AT.

2. Look for bent or damaged pins on DIP memory chips and SIP modules using a strong light and a magnifying glass. If a chip or module has a bent pin, remove it, straighten the pin, then reinstall. In the case of damage, replace the chip or module.

3. If chip or module pins are not bent or damaged, press firmly on each chip or module to ensure they are properly seated.

4. Ascertain that memory chips or modules are of the correct type for your PC and that they have matching speeds.

5. Ensure that the notches on chips and modules are mated with the notches on the board.

6. With a memory add-on card (above board), pull it and then reinstall it, ensuring it is properly seated.

7. Use a diagnostic program such as Checkit to identify a faulty memory chip.

8. If you do not have a diagnostic program, identify a faulty chip by trial and error as described in the steps that follow.

   a. Taking the most simple case first, if your AT is fitted with two SIMM or SIP modules, power down and remove one of them, then power up, adjust the memory configuration, and see if the parity error message is repeated. If it isn't, then you know that the removed module is faulty. If the message is repeated, you must repeat the procedure with the other module. In the case of multiple SIMM or SIP modules, testing is simply an extension of the procedure. You must power down for each test.

b. With DIP memory, remove a bank at a time altering switch settings on an XT or setup choices on an AT, and when the bank with the bad chip is found you proceed to identify that chip. Do it by pulling a chip from an identified good bank and then replacing it with each chip in turn from the suspect bank until the error message is repeated. You must power down for each test.

9. Remove all the chips and take them to a computer service center for checking with specialized test equipment.

MEMORY REMOVAL

CAUTION

Discharge static electricity from your body before handling memory chips or memory modules.

1. On some PCs, DIP chips arc not always readily accessible; if you encounter this problem, remove any obstructing components such as adapter cards, cables, or drives. Most drives can be slid forward after removing the locking clamps. If you are still unable to access all the memory chips, you have no alternative but to remove the motherboard in the manner described in Section 2-9.

2. Remove a DIP chip by gently easing up one end with a thin-bladed screwdriver, then lever up from underneath the body of the chip. DIP chip extractor tools are available but you may find them difficult to use.

3. Remove a SIMM or SIP module by easing back the plastic spring clip at the notch end of the module and, while holding it back, firmly grip the module and pull it upwards from its socket.

4. Store the memory in a safe place.

MEMORY INSERTION

DIP Chips

1. Generally, new DIP chips tend to have the two rows of pins spread too wide to easily enter the slots in the socket. The purpose of this is so that when a chip is pushed into the mouth of a memory chip inserter, the pins are all bent inwards slightly,

thereby applying pressure to the inner sides of the inserter to prevent the chip from falling out. To insert a chip by hand, you must first close the pins slightly by performing the sub-steps that follow.

   a. Firmly hold the chip at each end between thumb and forefinger.

   b. Place one row of pins flat on a hard surface, then apply some pressure to cause the whole row of pins to bend slightly inwards.

   c. Repeat for the other side.

TIP Do not overdo this modification; only a degree or two of angular bend is required and it is best to carry out the procedure in small steps, checking the pin positions against sockets after each bend.

2. When inserting a DIP chip by tool or by hand, align the notches in the chip and the socket, then ensure that the pins are lined up with the slots in the socket.

3. Ease the pins at the notch end just into the socket, then slowly rotate the chip backwards so that the other pins engage in the socket slots. Next, confirm that the pins are properly located, then apply steady but gentle pressure until the chip is firmly home.

TIP If at any time real resistance is felt, remove the chip and try again. If continued difficulty is experienced, recheck the alignment of pins to socket slots. If the difficulty persists, try another chip; this often works and most times you will find the offending chip will insert easily into another socket position.

4. Repeat steps 1 through 3 for all chips you are replacing.

5. Check all replaced chips for proper insertion using a strong light and, preferably, a magnifying glass.

6. In the event of locating a chip with a bent pin, remove the chip and carefully straighten the pin using fine-nosed pliers, then reinsert taking extreme care to ensure that the damaged pin enters its slot properly.

7. If you removed the motherboard, replace it by following the procedure in Section 2-9. With an XT set the dipswitches to suit the new memory, then, with an XT or an AT, connect the keyboard, monitor, and power cable, and power up. With an AT, enter setup where, with most BIOS makes, the new memory configuration will have been recorded automatically. Otherwise set the memory from the keyboard.

8. Following power up with an XT, or the automatic reboot on exiting setup with an AT, observe that the memory test is satisfactory.

9. Power down, replace the cover on your PC, and reconnect all cables.

SIMM and SIP Modules

1. Align the notches in module and socket, then use a thin-bladed screwdriver to hold back the plastic spring clip at the notch end of the socket and, while holding back the clip, insert the module pins into the socket slots, leaning the module slightly forward as you do it.

2. Ensure that all the pins are in their slots, then apply firm downward pressure as you bring the module to the vertical. When the module is properly seated the clip, when released, should spring into its locking position.

3. Connect the keyboard, monitor, and power cable, then power up and enter setup where, with most BIOS makes, the new memory configuration will have been recorded automatically. Otherwise set the memory from the keyboard.

4. Following the automatic reboot on exiting setup, observe that the memory test is satisfactory.

5. Power down, replace the cover on your PC, and reconnect all cables.

PREVENTIVE MAINTENANCE

- Maintain a well-ventilated and clean environment.
- Tune in to the operating sounds of your power supply, and if you hear a change, have the voltages checked by a competent technician.

Section 2-9

MOTHERBOARDS AND
THE BIOS

OVERVIEW

You will be extremely unlucky if you have need to replace a motherboard for reasons other than upgrading. Inherently, a printed circuit board with installed solid state components is not inclined to failure under normal operating conditions once it has been "burned in"—a procedure adopted by most computer manufacturers/assemblers. Burning in consists of operating the computer for some fixed period of time on the principle that if anything is likely to go wrong it will do so within the first few hours.

The most likely cause of motherboard failure would be if it is "fried" by a major power surge such as that caused by a lightning strike. In that event, other components in your computer will probably be damaged, particularly the power supply and the memory, and your recovery action is likely to be a trip to your local computer store looking for a bargain PC replacement—a possibility that underscores the need to install an efficient surge protection device.

Under conditions less drastic than a lightning strike, you determine the motherboard is at fault largely by trial and error. Since it is the last item to come under suspicion, you will have checked other components such as the power supply, memory, and possibly the BIOS, and come to the sad conclusion you have a faulty motherboard.

BIOS problems, fortunately, are also few and far between and more often than not are related to inconsistencies in the operation of some software applications and networking programs.

107

BIOS failure on a motherboard will result in a power-up failure and would be one of the "suspects" before resorting to motherboard replacement.

PROBLEMS AND RESPONSES

Problem Your PC fails to commence power-up and you have determined all cables are properly connected and the fan in the power supply is running.

Response Although a running fan is not 100% proof that a power supply is not faulty, it is close to it; therefore, you must suspect either the BIOS or the motherboard itself. Your BIOS can be tested professionally, or you can endeavor to borrow a set of similar BIOS chips to try out on your motherboard. In the latter case, if your PC powers up, you know that the old BIOS was faulty; if it does not power up, then you know your motherboard is faulty. There are commercial undertakings that offer to repair printed circuit boards and you may want to consider that approach. But, more than likely, if you have a motherboard failure, your PC will either still be under warranty or so old that an upgrade is the best option. When purchasing a motherboard, be sure that the memory chips you already have are compatible with the new board, or purchase new memory to suit. If you buy a 386 or 486 board via mail order, be sure the price you are quoted includes the CPU. A number of suppliers often quote prices for motherboards without CPU and you have to look at the fine print to find out.

BIOS REMOVAL

BIOS chips, measuring approximately 1.5-inches by 0.5-inches, are seated side by side, often between the expansion slots and memory banks on an AT motherboard. Most are marked with the maker's name, such as Phoenix, AMI, or Award. They are also marked as being "odd" and "even"—one of each, or they have similar reference numbers except for the last digit which will be odd on one, and even on the other.

1. Identify the two BIOS chips on your motherboard.

2. Label the motherboard next to each chip so that after they are removed you will be able to identify which socket is for the odd chip and which for the even chip.

3. Carefully pry up one end of a chip slightly, using a thin-bladed screwdriver.

4. Leave the screwdriver in position, then repeat at the other end with a second screwdriver.

5. Grip the ends of the chip between forefinger and thumb and ease it out of its socket.

6. Repeat steps 1 through 4 for the second chip.

BIOS REPLACEMENT

1. Offer a chip to the socket to determine if the pins match the socket slots. If they are too wide, you will need to adjust them in the same manner as was described for a DIP chip under Memory Insertion in Section 2-8.

2. With the chip and socket notches matched and the chip held almost horizontally, ease the pins at the lower end into the socket, then gently press the remaining pins into place. Check both sides as you do this, stopping if you see a pin bending. Straighten a bent pin carefully, using fine pliers.

3. Most times, the existing keyboard BIOS chip will work with the new ones. However, be prepared to make a replacement if you have keyboard problems after replacing the main BIOS.

4. Proceed with the reassembly and testing of your PC in accordance with the instructions given in Section 2-14.

MOTHERBOARD REMOVAL

With the disassembly procedures outlined in Section 2-4 accomplished, perform the steps that follow.

1. Orient the computer case so that the left side is towards the front of the work table. Disconnect any internal cables attached to adapter cards, labeling them for subsequent ease of recognition.

2. Remove the end locking screws from all cards and store in a safe place.

3. Grasp a solid part of a card firmly between thumb and fingers, avoiding sharp wire ends on the back and fragile devices on the front, then withdraw it. Repeat for all cards and place them in a safe place, labeled for later identification if necessary.

4. If you are using an external CMOS support battery, disconnect it from the motherboard.

5. Disconnect the power supply cables from the motherboard.

TIP Most power supply connectors have a centrally located plastic spring clip on one side of the connector which must be eased away from the socket on the motherboard before you can disconnect.

6. On Turbo XT and AT boards, disconnect the control panel cables from the motherboard.

7. Remove the screws from the metal hex posts (these posts, not visible until the motherboard is removed, are illustrated at Figure 2-9/1 later in this section). Place the screws in a safe place—you may need them for the new board.

8. While facing the left-hand side of the computer case, slide the board towards you until it will lift out.

TIP Most likely you will not find step 6 easy to achieve because the plastic stand-offs tend to snag. Try jiggling the board until it moves to the necessary position for lifting off. As a last resort you might try squeezing closed the expanding arms of the plastic standoffs, one at a time, and pulling the board off them.

9. If you plan on reusing the memory chips/modules, remove them from the motherboard by performing the steps previously described under Memory Removal in Section 2-8. Store the memory in a safe place.

10. If you plan to discard the old motherboard, you may wish to consider removing the BIOS and keyboard BIOS chips, and even the CPU if it is not soldered in, for possible future replacement value.

MOTHERBOARD REPLACEMENT

The first step, populating the memory banks, is carried out before the motherboard is installed in order to simplify matters. If the board is installed first, there may well be drive bay hardware, or other impediments, that make memory installation difficult.

1. Populate the required number of memory bank(s) on the motherboard (for this procedure refer to Memory Insertion in Section 2-8).

2. Following population, check carefully under a strong light, using a magnifying glass if available, to ensure that each chip or module is properly inserted and, in the case of DIP and SIP type RAM chips, that none of the pins are bent.

3. Hold the motherboard so that the expansion slots are to the left. Next, offer the motherboard to the case and identify the best positions for the insertion of the plastic stand-off supports and the locations of the metal hex posts. See Figure 2-9/1.

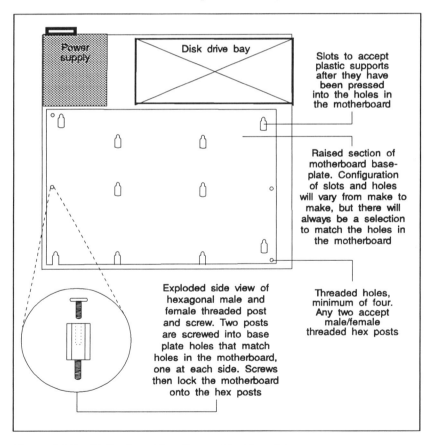

Figure 2-9/1—Motherboard locating and locking slots

4. Insert the plastic supports into the motherboard (see Figures 1-2/3 and 1-2/4 in Section 1-2).

5. Identify screws for at least two metal hex posts, then screw the posts into the appropriate places on the raised base plate of the case. Tighten with pliers or wrench.

6. Refer to the user manual that came with the motherboard and set all jumpers and/or dipswitches to conform to the chosen computer configuration. Identify the jumpers and connectors that will interface to the motherboard, the control panel LEDs and buttons, and the speaker.

7. Position the motherboard just above the raised base plate of the case, about half an inch back from its ultimate position, then lower it so that the plastic supports drop into the wide parts of the slots in the base plate. Work the board forward until the threaded holes of the metal hex posts can be seen through the appropriate holes in the motherboard. When the board is correctly located the keyboard interface will be lined up accurately with the round hole in the back wall of the case. Using a Phillips screwdriver, secure the board in position using the previously identified screws (see step 5 above).

8. Proceed with the reassembly and testing of your PC in accordance with the instructions given in Section 2-13.

PREVENTIVE MAINTENANCE

- Maintain a well-ventilated and clean environment.
- Tune in to the operating sounds of your power supply, and if you hear a change, have the voltages checked by a competent technician.

Section 2-10

FLOPPY DISK DRIVES

OVERVIEW

Unfortunately, floppy disk drive problems are likely to occur more frequently than hard disk problems, mainly because of the repeated physical action of inserting and removing floppy diskettes, and because diskettes are used interchangeably between drives of different specifications.

If after various tests you reach the conclusion that the disk drive is faulty beyond repair, try replacing the ribbon cable before investing in a new drive.

Problems can result from internal causes such as a misaligned head, failed circuitry, etc., which most users cannot correct. However, before you send the drive to a service company for repair, obtain a firm quote and then compare with replacement cost. You will probably find that for less money you can get a new drive—a much better deal than a repaired one which, of course, is still an old drive and may be susceptible to other failures.

PROBLEMS AND RESPONSES

Problem   Your floppy disk drive will not read or write, or you have a noisy drive that frequently displays Retry messages.

Response

1. Replace the diskette with another formatted one and retry. If the diskette reads, then the first one is faulty. Discard it unless it

contains data you need, in which case attempt disk recovery as described in Section 2-3.

2. Check the power cable and the ribbon cable connections.

3. Run a diagnostic program.

4. On an XT, check the dipswitches on the motherboard. On an AT, rerun setup.

5. If you have two daisy-chained floppy disk drives installed, be sure that drive 2 has the terminating resistor removed. These resistors vary in design and location on the drive. Figure 2-10/1 shows an example.

6. Reseat the controller card.

7. Clean the read/write head by following the procedures under CLEANING FLOPPY DISK DRIVE HEADS in the next subsection.

8. Replace the ribbon cable and controller card.

9. Replace the drive.

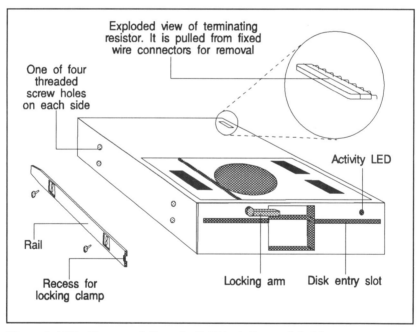

Figure 2-10/1—Representation of a 5.25-inch floppy disk drive

Problem Your XT floppy disk drive will read some diskettes but not others.

Response A common failure on an XT machine is inability to read a 1.2MB diskette that has been formatted on an AT machine using the /4 qualifier. The reason for this is that the 1.2MB drive on the AT machine normally formats 80 narrow tracks on a 5.25" diskette, and when you use the /4 qualifier it formats 40 narrow tracks widely spaced. A 360k drive formats 40 wide tracks, and when it tries to read the AT formatted diskette, it often does not center the head properly over the unexpectedly narrow track. Always ensure that the diskettes you wish to use have been formatted on an XT machine or by using software on an AT machine that simulates XT formatting.

CLEANING FLOPPY DISK DRIVE HEADS

1. Purchase a disk drive cleaning kit from your local computer dealer.

2. Apply the cleaning fluid supplied to the cleaning disk supplied.

3. With the computer running, insert the cleaning disk into the drive as you would a regular diskette.

4. Type **DIR <Enter>** to activate the drive motor and to cause the disk to rotate.

5. When the "Abort, Retry, Fail." message is displayed, type **R** to cause further rotation. Repeat twice more.

6. Remove the cleaning disk, insert a formatted diskette, and type **DIR** to test the drive.

FLOPPY DISK DRIVE REMOVAL

1. Disconnect the 4-pin power supply cable.

2. Disconnect the ribbon cable.

3. Remove the clamps from the front of the drive bay that lock the drive into the bay, retaining them for the replacement drive.

4. Slide the drive out of the bay on its rails.

5. Remove the rails and/or the 3.5" adapter from the drive, retaining them for the replacement drive. (See previous Figure 2-10/1 and the following Figure 1-10/2.)

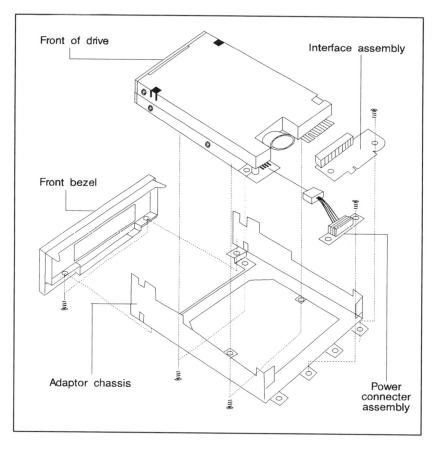

Front of drive

Interface assembly

Front bezel

Adaptor chassis

Power connecter assembly

Figure 2-10/2—3.5-inch drive ready for installation in an adapter

FLOPPY DISK DRIVE INSTALLATION

1. Replace the rails and/or the 5.25" adapter that you removed from the old drive.

2. If the drive is to be the second drive of a daisy-chained pair, remove the terminating resistor if one is installed.

3. Slide the drive into the bay along the drive bay rail guides and secure it in position with the drive clamps you reserved after removing the old drive.

4. Reconnect the 4-pin power supply cable and the 34-pin floppy drive ribbon cable coming from the controller card.

5. For an XT, set the dipswitches on the motherboard to suit the new drive if it is different from the old one. Next, boot the computer. For ATs, you must then enter the setup program in order to record details of the new floppy disk drive if it differs from the old one.

6. Test the drive by reading and writing to a formatted diskette.

PREVENTIVE MAINTENANCE

- Maintain a well-ventilated and clean environment.
- Avoid jarring your computer, particularly when the drive is working.
- Insert and remove diskettes carefully.
- Do not insert damaged diskettes.
- When moving your PC, insert a cardboard dummy disk or an old diskette to protect the head.

Section 2-11

HARD DISK DRIVES

OVERVIEW

A failing hard disk drive can emit what is obviously a dangerous noise, such as heavy grinding. If this happens and you have important data on the drive that has not been backed up, make copies as soon as possible and then power down. The cause can be either a failing drive or a faulty power supply.

If you experience hard disk failure, observing the "Don't panic" ground rule stated at the beginning of Section 2-1 now becomes important. A "disk failure" message does not necessarily mean "disk destruction."

A hard disk crash results from the read/write head making physical contact with a platter and can be caused by mishandling, particularly while the computer is running, and by power surges resulting from electrical storms or other phenomena.

Heavy hard disk fragmentation and lost clusters generally do not cause problems, however, periodically running a defragmentation program and the DOS CHKDSK is good practice. Particularly run CHKDSK if your PC powers down for any reason while you have an open file, but do not be too optimistic about recovering the file unless the particular application program you were running has automatic file saving capability.

CHKDSK

This DOS command exposes lost clusters—those lost when your PC is turned off while a file is open, causing the loss of the "pointer" DOS uses to track files. When running CHKDSK, do it first without the /F qualifier in order to determine if there are lost clusters. If there are, and if you have lost files you would like to try to save, first run a DIR and do a print screen, then run CHKDSK again with the /F qualifier (F for "fix"). If DOS reports it has found lost clusters in certain chains, it will ask if you wish to convert the chains to files. If you are not attempting recovery, answer with an N, otherwise answer with a Y. The files in the lost chains will then be written to disk as FILEnnnn.CHK, where nnnn is the file's number. The first file would be FILE0000.CHK, the next FILE0001.CHK, and so on. If the lost files were text files, examine them in a text editor; for files with other extensions, examine them in their original application program. You may be fortunate in recovering at least part of a lost file(s).

PROBLEMS AND RESPONSES

Problem   Your PC displays the message "Invalid drive specification," or "Disk not **found**," or similar.

Response

1. On an AT run the setup program to ensure the settings are correct.
2. On an XT check the dipswitches for the correct settings for your hard disk.
3. On both ATs and XTs ensure that the power cable from the power supply is properly interfaced with the hard drive.
4. Ensure that the control and data cables are properly interfaced with both the hard drive and the controller card.
5. Ensure that the controller card is properly seated in its bus-slot.
6. Run a diagnostic program such as Checkit.
7. Use a disk recovery program such as PC Tools.

119

Problem Your AT displays the bootup message "Invalid Con-figuration Information," followed by the message "Hard Disk Failure."

Response

1. More than likely the internal battery is dead, and since you have no way to test it, you should buy and fit an external battery holder and batteries (external from the motherboard—usually fixed to the side of the power supply with Velcro). These batteries and holder, which are inexpensive, have leads which interface with uncapped jumpers on the motherboard, usually near the original battery. Refer to your PC user manual for exact location.

2. Run a diagnostic test on the drive's controller card. If faulty, have it repaired or replace it, making your choice on cost basis.

Problem Your PC displays the message "Seek error, Abort, Retry, Fail." soon after booting.

Response

1. The most likely cause is over voltage from your power supply, which can cause the disk drive motor to overheat soon after booting. Have the voltages checked.

2. Run a diagnostic test.

HARD DISK DRIVE REMOVAL

1. If you are able to, back up your hard disk drive before removing it.

2. Disconnect the 4-pin power supply cable.

3. Disconnect the 34-pin controller and the 20-pin data ribbon cables.

4. Remove the clamps from the front of the drive bay that lock the drive into the bay, retaining them for the replacement drive.

5. Slide the drive out of the bay on its rails.

6. Remove the rails and/or the 3.5" adapter from the drive, retaining them for the replacement drive.

HARD DISK DRIVE INSTALLATION

1. In the unlikely event that your new drive is supplied with an installed front panel housing an LED light, as used in early PCs, remove it unless you have an early PC that requires the panel.

2. If the replacement drive is a 3.5" and your drive bay is 5.25", install the new drive into the 5.25" adapter that should have been supplied with the drive, together with installation instructions. Figure 1-2/11 in Section 1-2 illustrates a typical adapter.

3. Fit rails either to the drive or to the adapter frame, but position them so that the front of the drive is flush with the front of the drive bay and not the front panel of the computer. For ATs and most XTs, the intention here is that the drive will not be visible when the computer is fully assembled, and drive activity will be indicated by the LED on the computer control panel. In the case of older PCs, install it so that the supplied panel with the LED activity light fills the opening at the front of your PC.

4. Except in the case of an early PC, the drive may be installed in any bay. The left-hand bay (if there is one) is often the most convenient from the point of view of providing easy access to the connectors at the back of the drive. In most PCs, if the hard disk drive is located below the floppy disk drive(s), the hard disk drive connectors can be difficult to reach in the restricted space created by the position of the power supply.

5. Secure the drive in position with the drive clamps you reserved after removing the old drive.

6. Reconnect the 4-pin power supply cable and the 20-pin and 34-pin hard drive ribbon cables from the controller card.

7. For an XT, set the dipswitches on the motherboard to suit the new drive. Next, for XTs and ATs, insert a DOS boot disk into drive A and boot the computer. For ATs, you must then enter the setup program in order to record details of the new hard disk drive. Figure 2-2/2 in this section illustrates a typical setup program.

8. Proceed to INITIALIZING in the next subsection.

INITIALIZING

With the exception of hard disks with an IDE interface which have been factory preinitialized, hard disks are supplied with the platter surfaces not prepared for DOS formatting, and they must be initialized (also known as a low-level format).

CAUTION
Attempts to initialize an IDE hard disk may result in permanent destruction of the disk.

The following paragraphs describe the methods used to initialize hard disk drives.

Programs supplied with hard disk drives or controllers. Some hard disk drives are supplied with floppy diskettes containing initializing instructions, and you should follow the instructions.

Proprietary programs. Disk Manager or Speedstor are examples. Most computer stores carry such proprietary initializing programs.

The DOS DEBUG program with ATs. Used in conjunction with the program built into the BIOS setup utility or, for interfaces such as RLL, the program built into the hard disk controller's ROM. You should follow instructions after invoking setup.

The DOS DEBUG program with XTs. Used in conjunction with the program built into the hard disk controller's ROM, and you do this by performing the steps that follow.

1. Insert a DOS boot diskette in drive A and power up.

2. Insert into drive A the DOS diskette containing the DEBUG program.

3. Type **DEBUG <Enter>** to display the DEBUG program cursor (-).

4. Type **G=C800:5** or whatever the hard drive controller manual directs.

5. Generally speaking, you can answer screen questions with the affirmative by pressing **<Enter>**, including warnings about losing current data.

6. When your hard disk is initialized, proceed to the next subsection, FORMATTING.

FORMATTING

1. After successful initialization, with the computer running and a boot diskette in drive A, type **FDISK <Enter>**. In addition to a descriptive heading, the following will appear on your screen:

```
1. Create DOS partition or logical DOS drive
2. Set active partition
3. Delete DOS partition or logical DOS drive
4. Display partition data

Enter choice: [1]
```

A DOS partition provides space for the operating system as well as for user programs and data. Because a hard disk can hold more than one type of operating system at the same time, more than one partition can be created if needed. Furthermore, partitioning is necessary if you are using some early versions of DOS. For example, with version 3.3 DOS only recognizes 32MB at a time, and with a disk larger than 32MB you must divide it into one or more 32MB partitions which you will name C, D, E, etc. Versions 4.01 and up allow a single partition of any size. The early versions 2.0 to 3.2 do not recognize hard disks larger than 32MB.

2. Make your choice, then **<Enter>** and the next screen appears.

```
1. Create primary DOS partition
2. Create extended DOS partition
3. Create logical DOS drive(s) in the extended DOS
   partition

Enter choice: [1]
```

3. Make your choice, normally a primary partition, then **<Enter** and the next screen appears.

```
System will now restart
    Insert DOS diskette in drive A:
    Press any key when ready...
```

4. Press any key and your PC reboots automatically.

5. After the system has rebooted on the floppy diskette and the time and date have been bypassed (time and date always appears when booting from a floppy disk), at the A> prompt type **Format c: /s** **<Enter>** (The /s is a qualifier that tells the DOS FORMAT program to also transfer the system files from the floppy to the hard disk, thereby making the hard disk bootable—see the note following this instruction). The screen now displays:

```
WARNING. ALL DATA ON
NON-REMOVABLE DISK
DRIVE C: WILL BE LOST!
Proceed with Format (Y/N)?
```

NOTE

The system files are IO.SYS, MSDOS.SYS, and Command.com. The first two are hidden files—that is, they are not seen when a directory of files on a disk is requested. If they are not present on a boot disk, the boot fails, resulting in the message:

```
Non-System disk or disk error
Replace and strike any key when ready
```

In addition, if DOS cannot find the Command.com file, the following message is displayed:

```
Bad or missing Command Interpreter
```

6. Type **Y** and **<Enter>** to cause the DOS FORMAT program on the DOS floppy diskette to format the hard drive which is designated 'C.' Format percentage completed is displayed until 100% is reached, then the **Format complete** message will appear and, after a pause, **System transferred**, followed by **Volume label (11 characters, Enter for none)?**

7. All disks can be labeled, as volumes of books can be named, and DOS provides up to 11 characters for this name. If a volume label is desired, type in the chosen name at this point and then **<Enter>**; otherwise just **<Enter>**. Next, the following appears with the x's shown on this page representing actual numbers on the screen—numbers that vary according to disk size.

```
xxxxxxx        bytes total diskspace
xxxx           bytes used by system
xxx            bytes in bad sectors
xxxxxxx        bytes available on disk

xxx            bytes in each allocation unit
xxx            allocation units available on disk

Volume Serial Number is xxx xxx
```

Disks that hold the system files are given a serial number by DOS.

If you partitioned your drive for any reason, each partition must be formatted and will become known by the next following letter, i.e., D, E, F, etc.

8. Restore to your new hard disk drive the files from the most recent backup of your old drive. If you have no files to restore and you are uncertain of how to set up your new hard disk drive, proceed to DIRECTORIES & FILES in Section 4-3.

PREVENTIVE MAINTENANCE

- Maintain a well-ventilated and clean environment.
- Avoid jarring your computer, particularly when the hard disk is working.
- If you do not have a self-parking hard disk, use a parking program when you power down.
- Back up your hard disk regularly to protect data in the event of failure.
- If you are exposed to viruses via other people's floppies, networking, modem connections, etc., use an antivirus program.

Section 2-12

ADAPTER CARDS

OVERVIEW

Being solid state, adapter cards tend to give little trouble once installed properly. Any problem that does occur is likely to be with a card that has installed memory, or as a result of conflict with a newly installed card. Conflicts that occur when two cards try to use the same address or interrupt can be corrected by changing switches or jumpers on one of the cards.

Because there are so many different adapter cards, it would be difficult in this section to follow the format of previous sections which use Problem and Response headings. Accordingly, Sample Problem and Response headings will be used, and you must adopt the response principle of these examples as a strategy for solving other conflict problems you may experience.

PROBLEMS AND RESPONSES

Sample

Problem   Your PC already has a video card with a printer port, and after installing a multi-I/O card (a game port, a printer port, and two communication ports), your printer will not function.

Response   Because the default printer setting on your new multi-I/O card is for LPT1, and the printer port on your video card is also LPT1, you have a classic conflict. Two devices (even when not actively being used) are trying to use the same resources. Correct the problem by referring to the user manual for the new card and resetting the switches or jumpers to make the parallel port LPT2.

Problem   Your PC has a single serial port which is COM1 and which you use for a plotter connection. You install a new serial card to use with an external modem but neither device works.

Response   Same as the previous problem. Both ports are trying to use the same resources. Refer to the user manual for the new serial card and reset the switches to make it COM2, then configure your external modem for use with COM2 (the default is usually COM1).

More complex cards, such as those for plotters or scanners, can be difficult to set up unless they provide automatic or software setups. If not, you may need to use a diagnostic program to determine exactly which address and interrupt resources you are already using, and then configure the new device accordingly, using the device's user manual as a reference. Appendix B lists typical I/O addresses, Figure 1-2/14 in Section 1-2 illustrates IRQs on an AT, and Figure 2-12/1 that follows shows the results of the DOS MEM /DEBUG|MORE command.

```
Address      Name         Size      Type
-------      --------     ------    ------
000000                    000400    Interrupt Vector
000400                    000100    ROM Communication Area
000500                    000200    DOS Communication Area

000700       IO           000A60    System Data
             CON                    System Device Driver
             AUX                    System Device Driver
             PRN                    System Device Driver
             CLOCK$                 System Device Driver
             A: - C:                System Device Driver
             COM1                   System Device Driver
             LPT1                   System Device Driver
             LPT2                   System Device Driver
             LPT3                   System Device Driver
             COM2                   System Device Driver
             COM3                   System Device Driver
             COM4                   System Device Driver

001160       MSDOS        0013D0    System Data
 |-- More --
```

```
002530       IO            0120B0      System Data
             HIMEM         0004A0      DEVICE=
             XMSXXXX0                  Installed Device Driver
             SMARTDRV      005F40      DEVICE=
             SMARTAAR                  Installed Device Driver
             SETVER        000190      DEVICE=
             SETVERXX                  Installed Device Driver
             STACKER       00A340      DEVICE=
             D:                        Installed Device Driver
                           0006F0      FILES=
                           000100      FCBS=
                           000200      BUFFERS=
                           0001C0      LASTDRIVE=
                           000BC0      STACKS=
0145F0       MSDOS         000040      System Program

014640       COMMAND       000940      Program
014F90       COMMAND       000040      Data
014FE0       COMMAND       000400      Environment
0153F0       MSDOS         000040      -- Free --
015440       MOUSE         0042B0      Program
019700       MSDOS         0000A0      -- Free --
0197B0       SHARE         002030      Program
|-- More -

01B7F0       DOSSHELL      0000C0      Environment
01B8C0       MIRROR        001970      Program
01D240       DOSSHELL      000800      Program
01DA50       COMMAND       0000C0      Data
01DB20       COMMAND       000100      Environment
01DC30       MEM           0000B0      Environment
01DCF0       MSDOS         0009E0      -- Free --
01E6E0       GRAB          0000B0      Environment
01E7A0       GRAB          005C30      Program
0243E0       COMMAND       000940      Program
024D30       MEM           0176F0      Program
03C430       MSDOS         063BC0      -- Free --


    655360 bytes total conventional memory
    655360 bytes available to MS-DOS
    504512 largest executable program size

   3145728 bytes total contiguous extended memory
         0 bytes available contiguous extended memory
   2031616 bytes available XMS memory
           MS-DOS resident in High Memory Area

C:\>
```

Figure 2-12/1—Memory addresses

If you are short on interrupt lines, disable your LPT2 to free up IRQ 5, and even COM2 if you can spare it to free up IRQ 3.

If you need to make entries or changes in your AUTOEXEC.BAT and/or CONFIG.SYS, make copies of them beforehand—just in case.

ADAPTER CARD REMOVAL

1. With your PC powered down and the cover removed, disconnect any cables interfaced to the adapter card that is to be removed.

2. Remove the screw that locks the end cover of the adapter card to the back plate of the PC chassis.

3. Grip the card firmly and withdraw it from the bus connector.

ADAPTER CARD INSTALLATION

1. Ease the bronze colored connecting edge of the adapter card into the selected bus slot, then press firmly home.

2. Insert the screw that locks the end cover of the card to the back plate of the PC chassis.

3. Interface any required cables.

4. Check that all tools and other material are removed from the area of your PC, ensure that your monitor and keyboard are interfaced, plug in the power cable and power up.

5. Test the functionality of the card. If satisfactory, power down and replace the cover of your PC; otherwise perform the appropriate diagnostic checks to determine why it does not function.

Removing and installing an adapter card is a simple procedure under normal circumstances. However, here are some "tricks of the trade" you should be aware of.

- The bronze colored connector teeth on old cards may have become tarnished. A rubber eraser is an effective cleaning tool.

- When installing a card, grip it carefully but firmly, avoiding sharp wire ends on the back and fragile devices on the front.

- During installation, be sure the connectors are in the proper position relative to the bus. With several cards next to each other, it is not always apparent that you are seating a card properly, and all you may be doing is pressing it harder and harder to the side of a bus connector, possibly damaging electronic devices on the motherboard.

129

- The end plates on adapter cards are not always similar, and you may find the card will not install. Do not continue to try to seat the card until you determine if you must slightly bend the lower part of the end plate so that it mates with the slot in the PC's chassis.
- Install cards logically so that they are well-placed for the devices they serve.
- Avoid installing cards that run hot next to one another.

PREVENTIVE MAINTENANCE

- Maintain a well-ventilated and clean environment.
- Switch off your PC when not in use.

Section 2-13

CABLES

OVERVIEW

Cables that were manufactured some years ago lack the resilience to heat that modern cables have; as a result you should check old cables for flexibility, replacing them if they feel "brittle."

If you frequently remove the cover of your PC for one reason or another, replace any cables that have cut or abrasion damage, then tie cables so that they will not be snagged by the cover.

DRIVE CABLES

Power supply cables generally outlive the power supply. However, they can be difficult to interface with and/or disconnect from a drive, and care should be taken not to damage the wire connections. Do not pull on the cables to disconnect; if they are difficult to remove, use a wide-bladed screwdriver in the space between the white plastic male and female connectors, twisting the screwdriver to part the connectors.

Always replace a cable before replacing a drive if you are experiencing read/write problems; you might save time and money.

Route cables away from heat-generating chips on printed circuit boards, and so that they do not foul the computer case cover during its removal.

CONTROL PANEL CABLES

Unless it is obvious which cable interfaces with which jumper, label them before removal.

Route control panel cables, strapping them with plastic ties where necessary, to ensure they do not interfere with other components and so that they do not snag the computer case cover during its removal and replacement.

EXTERIOR CABLES

Ensure that all exterior cables are seated properly at each end. When securing screws or clips are provided, use them. Loose cables are a common source of computer problems and they can waste your time testing other components when attempting to troubleshoot.

Use ties to hold exterior cables together where feasible, and route them so that they are out of the way of feet and floor cleaning activities. Also, keep exterior cables away from heat sources such as radiators and hot air vents.

Section 2-14

REASSEMBLY AND TESTING

ASSEMBLY

Perform the steps that follow to put your PC back together.

1. Ensure that any component you have serviced or replaced is properly secured and, if it has cable connections, that they are properly made.
2. Remove all tools and leftover material from the PC and its vicinity.
3. Do not replace the PC case cover; just confirm that the main power switch on your PC is off, then connect the external power cable, the video cable, and the keyboard cable.

POWERING UP AND TESTING

1. Power up and, if the boot is successful, test the component you replaced, then power down again.
2. Make any other cable connections to peripherals and test your complete system.
3. If all is well, power down again, then replace the cover, securing it properly.

FAILED BOOT

1. If your PC fails to boot following the replacement of a component, recheck that any memory you have installed is properly seated, that all switch settings are correct, that the BIOS setup on ATs is correct, and that all cable connections are properly made.

2. Reboot, and if the problem persists, review the "Problem and Response" procedures that you followed after the original problem. It may be that you have replaced a component that was not faulty, leaving the faulty component still installed. For example, you may have replaced a good drive instead of a faulty cable, or a good BIOS instead of a faulty motherboard. Alternatively, you may have used a replacement part with the wrong specifications.

TIP If you are a rank amateur, do not despair. Even computer gurus sometimes experience difficulties after servicing their PCs. Think as a doctor thinks when he administers to a patient who did not respond to his first treatment: he goes over the symptoms again and again, and then he considers all of the possible medicines he can prescribe. Often there are so many possibilities that it's pure luck when he prescribes the right drug, whereas you, with your PC, are dealing with a limited number of possibilities. If you go through them one at a time, logically and carefully, you will come up with the right answer.

Usually, of course, the beginner has few problems because he or she carefully follows instructions, double-checking every move. It is the "experienced beginners" who make the mistakes by assuming that they know all the basics, but by skipping what they believe to be "kid's stuff" they fall into one of the many traps that the PC and its operating system always has ready for the unwary.

PART THREE

PERIPHERAL TROUBLESHOOTING AND REPAIRS

Section 3-1

MICE

OVERVIEW

The original Microsoft mouse, and other proprietary brands such as Logitech, were well-designed and constructed products likely to give long service. However, with price competitiveness dictating the market, other brands appeared at very low prices. With the low prices came poor design and short life.

Changes from the original basic design have also appeared in the marketplace; designs such as the roller-ball where the ball is on top of the mouse case and is rotated with the fingers or thumb. The roller-ball is very useful with portable computers where there is often no place to roll a mouse on a flat surface.

Another new design is the pen-mouse, where the mouse case is shaped like a fat pen, and a much smaller ball is located at the end. This type of mouse appeals to users who work a lot with draw and paint programs.

All mice tend to pick up foreign matter from the workplace, particularly dust and lint, which may cause malfunctioning of both the ball mechanism and electronic contacts.

PROBLEMS AND RESPONSES

Problem Your mouse cursor does not move properly across the screen as you move the mouse.

Response Remove the ball retaining clip and clean the ball with a pure cleaning alcohol. (At the same time, clean any electronic contacts that are accessible.)

Problem A button on your mouse does not function properly.

Response

1. If it is a cheap mouse, discard it and buy a new, better one.
2. If accessible, remove the screws holding the case together, then carefully separate the parts of the case to expose the electronic switches operated by the buttons. Clean the switches using a small stick-swab and pure cleaning alcohol. Reassemble and test. If the problem persists, replace the mouse.

PREVENTIVE MAINTENANCE

- Maintain a clean environment.
- Avoid operating your mouse on a cloth or paper surface that releases lint.
- If possible, use an authentic mouse pad.

Section 3-2

DIGITIZING BOARDS

OVERVIEW

Digitizing boards, once installed properly, tend to be trouble-free mainly because they have no moving parts, unlike a mouse where a ball moves. However, installation is often complicated and is frequently the cause of initial problems. Most times you must install very carefully, continually referring to user manual instructions. If you find installation too difficult, it pays to call the technical support department of the manufacturer directly, rather than the dealer who supplied it, unless the dealer is a specialist in the computer aided design market.

PROBLEMS AND RESPONSES

Problem   Your digitizer is unable to handshake with your PC. That is, communication between one and the other is not compatible.

Response

1. Reset the digitizer tablet dipswitches in accordance with the user manual instructions for your PC and for the CAD (or similar) program being used.

2. Check the user manual for your CAD (or similar) program for any references to the type of digitizing tablet you are using, and follow any directions given.

3. Seek help from the manufacturer's technical support department.

PREVENTIVE MAINTENANCE

- Maintain a clean environment.
- Cover the tablet and digitizer when not in use.
- Disconnect the power source if the digitizer is unlikely to be used for lengthy periods of time. Most digitizers use voltage regulators which tend to run hot.

Section 3-3

SCANNERS

OVERVIEW

Until the advent of the imaging industry, scanners were used primarily for scanning pictures for use in desktop publishing programs. There was some optical character recognition (OCR) scanning, but because of its generally poor degree of accuracy, it was not popular. More recently, with improvements in OCR software, scanning for data storage and retrieval has become a major industry, one that justifies its own magazine, "Imaging." As a result, there are more choices available of both scanners and software.

Despite all of these advances, scanners remain prone to failure because they employ moving parts and a light source in addition to printed circuit board electronics.

With most scanners, the PC/scanner/software combination must be matched. For example, there is scanning software that will only work with 386 machines, and there are scanners which will not function well with early PCs. When you purchase either a scanner or scanning software, be sure it will work with your PC.

Like many devices, a scanner usually interfaces to a PC via an adapter card which needs to be configured for memory and I/O addresses (see under Adapter Cards in Sections 1-2 and 2-12). Separate switches on the adapter card control the I/O address and the ROM memory address. Scanner adapter cards usually use parallel data transfer techniques, similar to a parallel printer card. Some scanners function without an adapter card, connecting directly to a serial port, but they tend to be slow.

PROBLEMS AND RESPONSES

Problem   Your scanner will not scan.
Response

1. Check all cable connections.
2. Check PC/scanner/software compatibility.
3. Check adapter card configuration.
4. Check that the light source within the scanner is functioning. If it is not, you may need professional help if the foregoing steps 1 through 3 check out.
5. With flatbed scanners, check that the light source moves when you give the scan command
6. Seek professional help.

Problem   The degree of accuracy of your OCR scanning is not acceptable.
Response

1. Ensure that the print you scan is well defined and, preferably, black on a white background.
2. Ensure that the print font you are scanning is within the capabilities of your scanning software. If not, and if your software is "trainable," follow the software user manual instructions on how to introduce a new font to the software.
3. Upgrade your scanning software.

Problem   There are smudges on the output from your flatbed scanner.
Response   Clean the glass.

PREVENTIVE MAINTENANCE

- Maintain a clean environment.
- Cover the scanner when not in use.

Section 3-4

PRINTERS

OVERVIEW

There are a vast number of printer makes and models, making it necessary for this section to be "general" in the broadest sense of the term. Repairing your own printer is a subject large enough to justify its own book.

Daisy wheel and dot matrix printers have large numbers of moving parts and therefore are more prone to failure than ink jets and lasers. Daisy wheel printers are rapidly becoming history because of a combination of excessive noise and slow speed, and they will not be covered in this chapter.

Ink jet printers are relatively new technology, and no pattern of failures has yet been established. Generally, they give good service although clogging of the jet nozzle may prove to be irksome.

True laser printers are largely trouble free from the hardware point of view. However, a solid state laser is likely to give better service than the helium/neon type. Since all laser printers use toner, under some circumstances it can escape from its cartridge and defile your printed sheets.

PROBLEMS AND RESPONSES

Problem   Your printer will not print.

Response

1. Check that the printer is switched on and is on line.

2. Check that your printer cables are properly connected.

3. Check your printer's control panel for error messages, and correct them as necessary.

4. Ensure that the active paper tray has paper.

5. Disconnect the printer cable at one end and then run the built-in self test. If it runs, you know the printer is OK and that the problem is PC, cable, or software related.

6. Ensure that the software and/or printer is properly configured for the type of software you are using and, particularly, that the proper printer driver is installed.

7. If you are using a software application program, exit the program and check to see if you can print a DOS screen. (Refer to the printer user manual and/or your DOS manual if you do not know how to do this.) If you can print a self test and a screen, then the problem is with your software. If you cannot print a DOS screen, the printer cable may be faulty—not an unusual occurrence.

8. If after completing the foregoing checks your printer still won't print, seek professional help.

PREVENTIVE MAINTENANCE

• Maintain a clean environment.

• Cover the printer when not in use.

• With a dot matrix machine, do not turn the platen by hand when the printer is switched on.

• With a laser printer, avoid spilling toner when you install a new cartridge.

• If you plan on using a rechargeable cartridge, be sure it is your original cartridge that is recharged, and have it recharged only once. Cartridges also have moving parts that can wear out.

• Remove the toner cartridge before shipping your printer anywhere.

• Regularly carry out any maintenance work recommended in the user manual.

Section 3-5

PLOTTERS

OVERVIEW

Like printers, plotters have a lot of moving parts, always an invitation to malfunctions; however, even with their many moving parts, the larger sizes of plotter are robust machines and hardware related failures are not common. Small plotters, like printers, are more prone to failure.

Unlike printers, there is basically only one type of plotter: a pen is moved by an arm in one direction, and paper or other media is moved by rollers in another direction 90 degrees to the pen movement. By varying the speed of each action, the pen can be made to reproduce any shape, and a lifting device raises and lowers the pen as required at the beginning and end of each part of a drawing, all automatically. With multiple pen plotters, the pen holder also changes pens automatically on command from software used in conjunction with a color monitor.

Plotters interface with PCs via a serial port, and cables may be serial, RS-232, or custom. Most plotters, like many printers, also have a control panel, but it is usually more complex because of the need to set up "handshaking" parameters such as parity (odd or even), number of data bits (7 or 8), number of stop bits (1 or 2), and protocol (the software/plotter communicating language). Almost all plotter problems relate to incorrect handshaking parameters. Small desktop plotters usually rely on dipswitches and not a control panel for setting parameters.

PROBLEMS AND RESPONSES

Problem   Your plotter will not plot.

Response

1. Check all cable connections.
2. Ensure you are using a plotter cable specified by the manufacturer.
3. Check that the control panel has been correctly configured for the work you are doing. (Handshaking parameters are usually configured from the control panel.)
4. Ensure that your application software supports your plotter make, or that you have instructed your plotter to emulate a supported plotter. (Most plotters emulate Hewlett Packard machines which are supported by all software.)
5. Disconnect the plotter from your PC and run its self-test program. If it plots, either the plotter cable is faulty or the handshaking parameters are set incorrectly.
6. Obtain professional help.

Problem   Your plotter only reproduces a portion of your drawing, as if the drawing is too large for the plotter.

Response   Check the software/plotter configuration to ensure that the correct plotting sizes have been selected.

Problem   Your plotter stops part way through reproducing your drawing.

Response   The byte size of your drawing exceeds the buffer size of your plotter, and either the plotter or the software is unable to refresh and continue. Refer to your plotter user manual for a solution or, if none is given, upgrade the buffer.

Problem Your plotter/software does not allow you to start a new drawing while another drawing is being plotted.

Response This is a case where the buffer control overrides PC control, preventing you from accessing your hard disk drive for the next job until the first is finished. If your plotter is compatible, consider buying a custom external floppy drive that attaches to the plotter. You then save a large drawing to a floppy diskette and place the floppy in the external drive where it "feeds" the plotter in buffer-size pieces, allowing you to commence the next drawing.

PREVENTIVE MAINTENANCE

- Maintain a clean environment.
- Cover the plotter when not in use.
- Regularly carry out any maintenance work recommended in the user manual.

Section 3-6
MODEMS

OVERVIEW

Whether modems are external or internal, they are solid state and tend not to suffer from hardware problems, although they do run hot. Internal modems are in effect a form of serial card, and care should be taken in setting the IRQ (interrupt jumper) so that it does not conflict with other devices. Appendix B lists typical I/O addresses, Figure 1-2/14 in Section 1-2 illustrates IRQs on an AT, and Figure 2-12/1 in Section 2-12 shows the results of the DOS MEM /DEBUG|MORE command. External modems connect to a serial port and must be set for an available port number.

Many problems that occur during modem connection to another modem are related to telephone line interference. Lightning strikes tend to find above ground telephone lines very easily, and if you are communicating with the West Coast from the East Coast, there are many miles of line and the possibility of many storms. A lightning strike to the telephone line that finishes up in your modem can get to your PC, so pay the price for an isolator, the modem equivalent of a surge suppresser.

Before using a modem for the first time, thoroughly acquaint yourself with the communications software you plan on using. More communication problems arise from misuse of the software than any other cause—similar to "garbage in, garbage out"—and keep in mind that the person at the other end of the connection must also be familiar with his software, which must be comapatible with yours.

PROBLEMS AND RESPONSES

Problem   Your modem is dead.

Response

1. Check cable connections.
2. With an external modem, check that it is switched on.
3. Recheck the setup of your telecommunications software package. Most are "picky" and must be set up perfectly.

Problem   You are unable to make a connection.

Response   Check the parameters (speed, parity, data bits, and stop bits).

PREVENTIVE MAINTENANCE

- Maintain a clean environment.
- Give an external modem air space to help ventilation.

PART FOUR
UPGRADES

Section 4-1

OVERVIEW

PLANNING AN UPGRADE CONFIGURATION

The PC purchased years ago for business or private use will still complete the tasks it was originally acquired for. However, since a fundamental business principle is that if the business is not growing it is dying, the likelihood is that the old PC can no longer manage the job efficiently. Also, in the private sector today, greater demands are made on the PC as people become more computer literate, using their PCs for home accounting and for accessing bulletin boards and services such as Compuserve and EasyLink. And, of course, we are all more impatient these days and seek those speed increases that new technology allows us to have in a modern PC. There is also the fact that many modern application software programs require a more powerful PC. For example, most advanced drawing programs will not run on an XT, requiring at least an AT286 and preferably a 386 with several megabytes of memory.

Fortunately, the structure of the PC is based on the principle of open architecture, which for the upgrader simply means you can add on, or upgrade, one component at a time.

Technology continues to advance, and although the blinding speed of the latest 486 machines makes one wonder if they can ever become faster, it's almost a certainty that they will. Likewise, software programs will continue to become more complex and therefore more demanding.

In the imaging sector of the computer industry massive amounts of data are handled, making speed of operation important. Storage capacity is also in demand; hence the growing use of large capacity optical disks and hard disks such as Digital's 5.25" with 3.5 gigabytes of formatted capacity.

It is propitious at this time that competition between manufacturers and value added resellers has forced retail prices down, helped along by more competition between makers of component parts. An excellent example is the appearance of new CPU brand names since Intel lost its monopoly of CPU copyrights. Even IBM, historically the most expensive manufacturer of PCs, is competing pricewise with "cheapy" clones and expanding their market outlets by supplying to department stores such as Montgomery Ward and superstores such as Bizmart. Upgrading your PC need not cost you a bundle, even though you should aim for an upgrade that will take you beyond your current needs. If your needs today have increased since yesteryear, they are likely to increase in the future. With this in mind, you should seriously consider upgrading as high as your budget will allow, almost disregarding your assessed needs for the present. If budget is a constraint, you can always do it step by step.

A step-by-step upgrade of a Turbo XT could proceed along the following lines, carrying out each step as your budget permits it.

- Power supply
- Switchable keyboard
- Motherboard with minimum memory
- Floppy drive(s)
- Hard drive and controller
- Memory above minimum

UPGRADING COMPONENTS

You upgrade a component for some specific need, and you do it within the capabilities of your existing PC. For example, if you have an XT and your power supply is noisy, you should consider upgrading it to an AT type in anticipation of a system upgrade at some future date. Using a higher rated power supply than is necessary has no adverse effects, since the motherboard and the drives only draw the watts they need.

If you decide you must be able to read 1.2MB floppy disks, you would normally plan on a full upgrade to an AT286—power supply, motherboard, memory, keyboard (possibly), hard drive controller (possibly), and floppy disk drive(s). However, as an alternative if dollars are tight, you might consider an XT motherboard fitted with the 12 MHz NEC V20 CPU that recognizes high density floppy disk drives—if you can find one. Although the ever decreasing price of 286 motherboards may make the savings look negligible, remember that with the NEC you do not need to upgrade the power supply, keyboard, and hard drive controller. Another benefit of the NEC V20 CPU is that its speed matches some of the slower 286 machines.

The simplest component upgrade is memory, providing you have unpopulated banks on your motherboard. If not, you must consider a memory expansion adapter card.

Upgrading the CPU alone is not recommended. Instead, an accelerator card should be used which boosts an XT to an AT. These devices, which plug into an 8-bit slot on the bus, have their own CPU as well as other electronic devices and circuits. However, you may still need to replace other components such as a floppy disk drive in order to get the benefit of high density diskettes, hard disk controller card, and possibly the power supply and keyboard. Accelerator cards are manufactured by such corporations as Intel, SOTA, and Cumulus.

UPGRADING AN XT TO AN AT

Upgrading a basic XT to an AT is generally not economically feasible because you end up replacing or adding to every component and maybe even replacing the case as well. Upgrading a turbo XT to an AT is one step better in that the control panel on the case may well be suitable for connection to an AT motherboard. In the list that follows, each component is discussed from the point of view of its compatibility with an AT motherboard.

- **Power Supply**—The wattage of a power supply is rated to suit its intended use, taking the watts the motherboard and drives demand and adding a "buffer" to cater for any expansion cards that may be added later. Early PCs required about 65 watts, XTs 130 watts, and ATs 190 watts. Power supplies are available in sizes of 135 watts (early PCs), 150 watts (XTs), 200 watts (ATs), 250 watts, and 330 watts, with

155

the higher ratings for PCs handling heavy tasks such as network file serving. If you are upgrading to an AT, you will expose your PC to risk if you use less that a 200-watt power supply.

- **Memory**—The DIP memory on your old XT is likely to have slow access time, i.e., 150 or 120 nanoseconds, and the chip size may be as little as 64K. Most ATs demand at least 256K chip sizes, often in SIMM or SIP configuration. Upgrading from XT to AT invariably calls for new memory.

- **Floppy Disk Drive**—Drives that accept 360K and 720K diskettes will function perfectly well in an AT, however, not to take advantage of high density drives would be wasteful. In any event, most new versions of major software application programs are supplied on high density diskettes. If you have been working with one floppy and one hard drive, you may wish to leave the low density drive installed and add a high density as a second drive.

- **Hard Disk Drive**—Most drives used in XTs will work in ATs. However, the odds are that your old XT drive is slow and short on storage capacity. Upgrading to a faster drive will be beneficial if you use your PC for anything more than word processing and data bases.

- **Disk Controller**—XT- and AT-type hard disk controller cards are, generally, not interchangeable. That is to say, if you upgrade your PC from XT to AT, you will almost certainly need to change the controller card even if you retain your old hard disk drive. The reason for this is that most XT-type controllers transfer data through Direct Memory Access (DMA) channels, whereas an AT-type controller stores data in 512K portions and then uses an Interrupt Request (IRQ) to get the AT CPU to read the data. When you purchase a new controller, be sure it is compatible with your hard disk drive type. In both XTs and ATs, separate controllers are available for both floppy and hard disk drives, or, in ATs, one controller can serve both types of drive. Incidentally, a floppy disk drive does not care what sort of controller it has, e.g., MFM or RLL. Finally, most modern XT controllers only permit 1:3 interleaving, while most AT controllers permit 1:1.

- **Keyboard**—If your XT keyboard is not switchable for use with an AT, you will need to replace it on upgrading from XT to AT. XT-type keyboards have the control chip in the keyboard, whereas with ATs the control chip is on the motherboard.

UPGRADING AN AT-286 TO AN AT-386 OR 486

Basically, there are no serious considerations in upgrading ATs; only the motherboard needs to be changed. However, when shopping for a new board try to find an acceptable one that uses the same type of memory that you have in your 286—and be sure the price includes the CPU.

The main considerations you will be faced with are speed, 386 or 486, SX or DX, and memory cache or not. In the list that follows each consideration is discussed.

- **Speed**—Speed is desirable in most applications, and there is not a great difference in retail price between an average 386-25DX motherboard and a 386-33DX, although the difference is more marked with 486s. Let the speed you choose be dictated by the applications you run. Whereas 25MHz is fine for word processing, the fastest available is never fast enough for imaging or CAD work.
- **386 or 486**—Since you should beware of low-cost motherboards, cost may have a bearing on your decision. However, assuming your budget can bear it, go for a good 486 motherboard on the basis that you will remain on the leading edge of technology for a while longer. In any event, go for a 486 board if your work involves activities such as desktop publishing, computer aided design, or heavy imaging.
- **SX or DX**—The SX has a data bus half the width of the 32-bit DX. This means that an SX CPU cannot handle internal data movement as fast as a DX, though they both output data at the same speed. Again, if you are involved in desktop publishing, computer aided design, or heavy imaging—activities which involve heavy internal computing—choose the DX board.

- **Cache or No Cache**—386 motherboards with cache ability cost more than those without. Cache memory is static RAM, as opposed to normal dynamic RAM. Static RAM is much faster than dynamic RAM, but it is also relatively expensive, which makes it prohibitive to use as regular PC RAM. 386 motherboards with cache memory use a cache controller located on the board, whereas with 486 motherboards the controller is in the CPU. 486 motherboards are available with 256K cache, and 386 boards with 64K. A cache controller speeds up operations by holding in cache memory information that relates to the work being done, thereby allowing the CPU to "dip" into the fast cache memory rather than going on to the relatively slow RAM memory. Once again, your decision will be based on your speed needs and your budget.

THE UPGRADE OR "BARE-BONES" PURCHASE DECISION

A bare-bones PC is a case, power supply, and motherboard—all assembled and tested at a price very little more than you would pay for the separate components. The best part of this deal is that you do not have to do the hard part, which is installing and connecting the motherboard. The bare-bones PC you receive will work as soon as you install memory, a floppy disk drive, and a video card, and hook it up to a keyboard and monitor.

XT TO AT UPGRADE   Nine times out of ten it will pay you to make the bare-bones choice because, even if your PC case is compatible with an AT motherboard, the case is sure to be showing signs of wear, and even if the power supply is of the right size, it too will be showing signs of wear.

AT286 TO AT386 OR 486 UPGRADE Basically, the only component to be upgraded is the motherboard (and possibly memory), and since your 286 case and power supply are likely to be relatively new, there is little to be gained from making the bare-bones choice unless you have a need for a different size or type of case.

Section 4-2

ADDING OR UPGRADING COMPONENTS OTHER THAN MOTHERBOARDS

MEMORY

You upgrade memory for one of two reasons: to increase the size of your PC's total RAM, or to increase the speed (access time) of your PC's RAM.

RAM SIZE Early PCs were supplied with 64K of RAM which, at the time, was more than adequate to run the software application programs that were then available. Over the years since the first PCs hit the marketplace, CPU and memory chip design have advanced both independently and in parallel with the needs of more advanced software application programs. Two or three years ago, AT286 PCs were mostly supplied with 1MB of RAM. Today, most users look for 2 MBs, and "power" users 4MBs and more. When deciding to upgrade RAM size you should consider only two aspects. The first is if you are getting "Insufficient memory" messages, and the second is if you are planning to add a software package that needs some given amount of memory which is more than you already have.

SPEED Access time is a measurement in nanoseconds (ns) of how long it takes a CPU to acquire information from RAM. A nanosecond is a billionth of a second. However, for a PC to be able to utilize the speed of its memory chips, the CPU must be just as fast. The speed of the memory chips supplied with your computer is likely to be the fastest the CPU can handle, and to upgrade to a faster chip would be pointless. Upgrading memory for speed is only feasible when you upgrade your motherboard to a faster speed. For example, when upgrading your 10MHz XT to a 16MHz AT286 you would need and benefit from faster memory chips, but when upgrading an AT386/33MHz PC to an AT486/33Mhx there would be no benefit in installing faster chips. (The foregoing assumes both PCs were originally fitted with the correct memory chips.)

Early memory chips were designed to have access times of 250 ns, then 200 ns. For the first XTs, 150 ns chips were designed, and 120 ns for later ones. When the AT appeared, chip access times were increased to 100 ns, then 80 ns, and even faster more recently. The user manual for a PC or for a motherboard will state desirable memory chip access time, possibly in a statement such as, "12.5 MHz at 0 wait state with 100 ns RAM."

CHIP SIZE   Early PCs used chips of 64K bits (bits, not bytes) and 128K bits. Most XTs use 256K bit chips, as do some early AT286 machines, with nine DIP chips giving 256K bytes of RAM (eight for the actual memory and one as the controller). Today, 1024K bit chips are more popular, in both DIP and SIMM packaging. 4096K bit SIMMs are also available. Some AT motherboards are designed to accept two sizes of DIP chips in the same bank: 256K bit and 1024K bit, and with four banks this provides an easy opportunity to upgrade memory from a minimum of 1MB to a maximum of 4 MB. Similarly, many SIMM sockets (also called banks) are able to accept either 1024K bit modules or 4096K bit modules. Also, some AT motherboards house a mixture of DIP and SIMM. There are rules to be followed, of course, usually prohibiting odd memory sizes such as three banks of nine 256K bit chips.

EXPANDED MEMORY CARDS   There are a number of makes of memory add-on cards, some cheaper than others, but you get what you pay for. Intel makes an excellent add-on known as the AboveBoard. An add-on card is little more than an adapter card with banks for DIP memory chips, and they come in a range of sizes suitable for both XTs and ATs.

The hardware side of the installation is simple, as for any adapter card (see the subsection headed ADAPTER CARDS later in this section). However, the software installation procedure, which varies with different makes, can be more demanding, and you should refer to the user manual that comes with the card.

REMOVING AND INSTALLING MEMORY CHIPS   From the steps that follow, you learn to remove and install DIP, SIMM, and SIP memory chips.

Memory Removal

CAUTION
Discharge static electricity from your body before handling memory chips or memory modules.

1. In the case of DIP memory chips, if any of them are not readily accessible, remove components and/or the motherboard in the manner described in Section 2-8 under the heading MEMORY REMOVAL.
2. Remove a DIP chip by gently easing up one end with a thin-bladed screwdriver, then lever up from underneath the body of the chip, or use a memory extractor tool.
3. Remove a SIMM or SIP module by easing back the plastic spring clip at the notch end of the socket and, while holding it back, firmly grip the module and pull it upwards from its socket.
4. Store the memory in a safe place.

Memory Insertion

DIP Chips

1. Generally, new DIP chips tend to have the two rows of pins spread too wide to easily enter the slots in the socket. The purpose of this is so that when a chip is pushed into the mouth of a memory chip inserter, the pins are all bent inwards slightly, thereby applying pressure to the inner sides of the inserter to prevent the chip from falling out. To insert a chip by hand, you must first close the pins slightly by performing the sub-steps that follow.
   a. Firmly hold the chip at each end between thumb and forefinger.
   b. Place one row of pins flat on a hard surface, then apply some pressure to cause the whole row of pins to bend slightly inwards.
   c. Repeat for the other side.

161

TIP Do not overdo this modification; only a degree or two of angular bend is required and it is best to carry out the procedure in small steps, checking the pin positions against sockets after each bend.

2. When inserting DIP chips by tool or by hand, align the notches in the chip and the socket, then ensure that the pins are lined up with the slots in the socket.

3. Ease the pins at the notch end just into the socket, then slowly rotate the chip backwards so that the other pins engage in the socket slots. Next, confirm that the pins are properly located, then apply steady but gentle pressure until the chip is firmly home.

TIP If at any time real resistance is felt, remove the chip and try again. If continued difficulty is experienced, recheck the alignment of pins to socket holes. If the difficulty persists, try another chip; this often works and most times you will find the offending chip will insert easily into another socket position.

4. Repeat for all chips.

5. Check all chips for proper insertion using a strong light and, preferably, a magnifying glass.

6. In the event of locating a chip with a bent pin, remove the chip and carefully straighten the pin using fine-nosed pliers, then reinsert taking extreme care to ensure that the damaged pin enters its slot properly.

7. If necessary, replace the motherboard and connect its cables. With an XT, set the dipswitches to suit the new memory, then, with an XT or an AT, connect the keyboard, monitor, and power cable, and power up. With an AT, enter setup, where with most BIOS makes, the new memory configuration will be recorded automatically. Otherwise set the memory from the keyboard. A typical setup program is shown at Figure 2-2/2 in Section 2-2.

8. Following power-up with an XT or the automatic reboot on exiting setup with an AT, observe that the memory test is satisfactory.

9. Replace the cover on your PC.

SIMM and SIP Modules

1. Use a thin-bladed screwdriver to hold back the plastic spring clip at the notch end of the socket and, while holding back the clip, insert the module pins into the socket slots, leaning the module slightly forward as you do it.

2. Ensure that all the pins are in their slots, then apply firm downward pressure as you bring the module to the vertical. When the module is properly seated the clip, when released, should spring into its locking position.

3. Repeat for all modules.

4. With the motherboard in place, connect the keyboard, monitor, and power cable, then power up and enter setup where, with most BIOS makes, the new memory configuration will be recorded automatically. Otherwise set the memory from the keyboard. A typical setup program is shown at Figure 2-2/2 in Section 2-2.

5. Following the automatic reboot on exiting setup, observe that the memory test is satisfactory.

6. Replace the cover on your PC.

FLOPPY DISK DRIVES

ADDING A FLOPPY DISK DRIVE   Perform the steps that follow to add any floppy disk drive as a second drive. If you do not have the second set of rails and drive clamps usually supplied with new PCs, you will need to acquire a set of each to suit the drive bay design of your PC. You can order rails and clamps when you order the drive, or pick them up from most computer stores.

1. If the drive is to be the second drive of a daisy-chained pair, remove the terminating resistor if one is installed.

2. To install a 3.5" drive into a 5.25" bay, first install it into the 5.25" adapter which should have been supplied with the drive. To achieve this, follow the instructions supplied with the adapter kit. If a kit was not supplied, you must order one.

3. For a drive you are installing into a 5.25" bay, fit rails to either the 5.25" drive or the adapter that houses the 3.5" drive. For a 3.5" drive being fitted into a 3.5" bay, follow the instructions in the user manual for the PC.

4. Slide the drive into the bay along the drive bay rail guides, and then secure it in position with drive clamps. If it is to be drive B, use the bay immediately below the first installed one so that the naming of the drives becomes logical with A on the top. If you intend your new drive to be drive A, and if you wish to follow the logical naming sequence, first remove the old drive and install it in the second bay down.

5. Connect a 4-pin power supply cable to your new drive, then interface the 34-pin floppy drive controller ribbon cable coming from the controller card so that the end connector goes to drive A, and the connector within the cable goes to drive B.

6. For an XT, set the dipswitches on the motherboard to suit the new drive. Next, for XTs and ATs, boot the computer. For ATs, you must then enter the setup program in order to record details of the new disk drive. A typical setup program is shown at Figure 2-2/2 in Section 2-2.

7. Test the drive by reading and writing to a formatted diskette.

UPGRADING A FLOPPY DISK DRIVE   You will only upgrade a floppy disk drive if you have an XT that you are upgrading to an AT, or you have an AT with one high density and one low density floppy disk drive and you have decided to discard the low density, upgrading it with a high density. Essentially, the procedure is the same as that outlined in the previous steps; however, if you are also upgrading an XT motherboard, you may wish to refer to the appropriate steps in Section 4-4.

HARD DISK DRIVES

Virtually any drive can be formatted with an MFM or RLL interface, although with the RLL interface you are advised to use a drive of good quality since the formatting procedure places greater demands on the disk drive. In any event, it has been said somewhere that cheap hard disk drives make good but expensive paperweights.

When you upgrade your hard disk you should make sure it will interface with your existing controller card, unless you plan to purchase a new controller card to match your new drive. Within the limitations of your budget, it is good practice to upgrade with a hard disk drive having a higher storage capacity than you foresee yourself needing, and one with the fastest access time available. When you have storage space to spare on an AT, some software application programs can convert a portion of the hard disk memory into a form of cache, accessible by the CPU at speeds greatly in excess of normal access time to RAM.

When purchasing a new hard disk drive as a second drive, be sure to order rails, drive bay clamps, and a 3.5"/5.25" adapter if your new drive is to be a 3.5" for installation into a 5.25" bay. You may also need a new 34-pin cable fitted with two drive connectors.

HARD DISK DRIVE REMOVAL   Perform the steps that follow to remove your old hard disk drive.

1. Disconnect the 4-pin power supply cable.
2. Disconnect the 20-pin and 34-pin ribbon cables.
3. Remove the clamps from the front of the drive bay that lock the drive into the bay, retaining them for the replacement drive.
4. Slide the drive out of the bay on its rails.
5. Remove the rails and/or the 3.5" adapter from the drive, retaining them for the replacement drive.

HARD DISK DRIVE INSTALLATION   Perform the steps that follow to install a new hard disk drive.

1. In the unlikely event that your new drive is supplied with an installed front panel housing an LED light, as used in early PCs, remove it unless you have an early PC that requires the panel.
2. If the new drive is a 3.5" and your drive bay is 5.25", install the new drive into the 5.25" adapter that should have been supplied with the drive together with installation instructions.
3. For installation of a 3.5" drive into a 3.5" bay, follow the directions given in your PC's user manual. Otherwise, fit rails either to the drive or to the adapter frame, but position them so that the front of the drive is flush with the front of the drive bay and not the front panel of the computer. For ATs and most XTs, the intention here is that the drive will not be visible when the computer is fully assembled, and drive activity will be indicated by the LED on the computer control panel. In the case of older PCs, install it so that the supplied LED panel fills the opening at the front of your PC.

4. The drive may be installed anywhere in the bays. The left-hand bay (if there is one) is often the most convenient from the point of view of providing easy access to the connectors at the back of the drive. In most PCs, if they are located below the floppy drive(s) the hard drive connectors will be difficult to reach in the restricted space created by the position of the power supply. If it is a second hard disk drive you are installing, locate it next to the one already installed in order to facilitate connecting the 34-pin cable. In such a case, you will need a 34-pin cable with two interface connectors and, if a terminating resistor is installed on the drive connected by the last cable connector, you must remove it.

5. Secure the drive in position with drive clamps reserved after removing the old drive or new ones if you are installing a second drive.

6. Reconnect the 4-pin power supply cable and the 20-pin and 34-pin hard drive ribbon cables from the controller card.

7. For an XT, set the dipswitches on the motherboard to suit the new drive. Next, for XTs and ATs, insert a DOS boot diskette into drive A and boot the computer. For ATs, you must then enter the setup program in order to record details of the new hard disk drive. A typical setup program is shown at Figure 2-2/2 in Section 2-2.

Refer to Section 4-3 for initializing and formatting procedures.

DISK CONTROLLER CARD

Perform the steps that follow to remove any disk controller card and to install a replacement.

1. Disconnect any cables attached to the card, if necessary labeling them for subsequent ease of recognition.

2. Remove the end locking screw from the card and store in a safe place.

3. Grasp a solid part of the card firmly between thumb and fingers, avoiding sharp wire ends on one side and fragile components on the other, then withdraw it.

166

4. Insert your new disk controller card into an appropriate slot near the drive bays, then screw it to the chassis back plate.

5. Interface the ribbon cables from the drives to the correct sockets on the card. See Figures 1-2/12 in Section 1-2.

POWER SUPPLY

Perform the steps that follow to remove and replace a power supply after disconnecting the main power cable from the wall outlet or surge protector.

1. Disconnect the 4-pin cables from any installed drives.

2. Disconnect the power supply cables from the motherboard.

TIP Most power supply connectors have a centrally located plastic spring clip on one side of the connector which must be eased away from the socket on the motherboard before you can disconnect.

3. Remove the screws from the back panel of your PC's chassis where they lock the power supply in position. Store them in a safe place.

4. Slide the power supply away from the back of the chassis until the tongue and slot locking device on the bottom of the power supply is released and the unit can be removed.

5. Position the new power supply so that you can slide the slot in the unit's base over the raised tongue on the computer chassis.

6. Secure the unit to the back of the computer chassis using the screws removed from the old power supply.

7. Identify the power supply connector with an orange cable at one end. Grip the connector so that the orange cable is nearest the back wall of the computer chassis and so that the connector itself is immediately above the end of the ribbon connector socket nearest the back wall of the computer case. See Figure 1-2/10 in Section 1-2.

8. Tilt the top of the connector away from the power supply and engage pegs on the connector with the small slots in the socket. Straighten the connector while pressing down to complete a secure interface. Repeat procedure for second connector.

9. Connect 4-pin power cables to installed drives.

10. Reconnect the main power cable.

VIDEO SUBSYSTEM

In order to obtain the best results with this subsystem, it is almost as important to match the monitor and the video card as it is to match a hard drive and its controller card. For more information on this subject, see Video Cards under the heading ADAPTER CARDS in Section 1-2, and MONITORS in Section 1-3.

To replace a monitor, power down your PC and simply disconnect the monitor power cable from its power source and the video cable from its port at the back of your PC, then connect the two similar cables of your new monitor.

To remove and install a video card, perform the steps that follow.

1. Power down your PC and remove its cover (see Section 2-4—DISASSEMBLY INSTRUCTIONS).

2. Disconnect the video cable from the card.

3. Remove the screw that locks the card's end cover to the PC's back plate.

4. Grip the card firmly between fingers and thumb, avoiding sharp wire ends on the back of the card and fragile devices on the front of the card, then remove it using a rocking motion if it does not pull easily.

5. Set any jumpers and/or switches on the new card according to instructions in the card's user manual for your type of monitor.

6. Press the card firmly into a suitable expansion slot on the motherboard, ensuring that the bronze-colored connector is in the right position.

7. Replace the screw that locks the end cover of the card to the back plate of your PC.

8. Interface the video cable to the card, screwing it in tightly.

9. Switch on your monitor and boot your PC.

Refer to Section 2-14 for reassembly procedures for your PC.

Section 4-3

SETTING UP A HARD DISK

INITIALIZING

With the exception of hard disks with an IDE interface which have been factory preinitialized, hard disks are supplied with the platter surfaces not prepared for DOS formatting, and they must be initialized (also known as a low-level format).

CAUTION
Attempts to initialize an IDE hard disk may result in permanent destruction of the disk.

The following paragraphs describe the methods used to initialize hard disk drives.

Programs supplied with hard disk drives or controllers. Some hard disk drives are supplied with floppy diskettes containing initializing instructions, and you should follow the instructions.

Proprietary programs. Disk Manager or Speedstor are examples. Most computer stores carry such proprietary initializing programs.

The DOS DEBUG program with ATs. Used in conjunction with the program built into the BIOS setup utility or, for interfaces such as RLL, the program built into the hard disk controller's ROM. You should follow instructions after invoking setup.

The DOS DEBUG program with XTs. Used in conjunction with the program built into the hard disk controller's ROM, and you do this by performing the steps that follow.

1. Insert a DOS boot diskette in drive A and power up.

2. Insert into drive A the DOS diskette containing the DEBUG program.

3. Type **DEBUG <Enter>** to display the DEBUG program cursor (-).

4. Type **G=C800:5** or whatever similar command the hard drive controller manual directs.

5. Generally speaking, you can answer screen questions in the affirmative (by pressing **<Enter>**) and OK warnings about losing current data. Initializing will then commence.

6. When your disk is initialized, proceed to the next subsection, FORMATTING.

FORMATTING

1. After successful initialization, with the computer running and the boot diskette in drive A, type **FDISK <Enter>**. In addition to a descriptive heading, the following will appear on your screen:

```
1. Create DOS partition or logical DOS drive
2. Set active partition
3. Delete DOS partition or logical DOS drive
4. Display partition data

Enter choice: [1]
```

A DOS partition provides space for the operating system as well as for user programs and data. Because a hard disk can hold more than one type of operating system at the same time, more than one partition can be created if needed. Furthermore, partitioning is necessary if you are using some early versions of DOS. For example, with version 3.3 DOS only recognizes 32MB at a time, and with a disk larger than 32MB you must divide it into one or more 32MB partitions which you will name C, D, E, etc. Version 4.01 and up allows a single partition of any size. The early versions 2.0 to 3.2 do not recognize hard disks larger than 32MB.

2. Make your choice, then **<Enter>** and the next screen appears.

```
1. Create primary DOS partition
2. Create extended DOS partition
3. Create logical DOS drive(s) in the extended DOS
   partition

Enter choice: [1]
```

3. Make your choice, normally a primary partition, then **<Enter>** and the next screen appears.

```
System will now restart
    Insert DOS diskette in drive A:
    Press any key when ready...
```

4. Press any key and your PC reboots automatically.

5. After the system has rebooted on the floppy diskette and the time and date have been bypassed (time and date always appears when booting from a floppy disk), at the A> prompt type **Format c: /s** **<Enter>** (The /s is a qualifier that tells the DOS FORMAT program to also transfer the system files from the floppy to the hard disk, thereby making the hard disk bootable—see the note following this instruction). The screen now displays:

```
WARNING. ALL DATA ON
NON-REMOVABLE DISK
DRIVE C: WILL BE LOST!
Proceed with Format (Y/N)?
```

NOTE

The system files are IO.SYS, MSDOS.SYS, and Command.com. The first two are hidden files—that is, they are not seen when a directory of files on a disk is requested. If they are not present on a boot disk, the boot fails, resulting in the message:

```
Non-System disk or disk error
Replace and strike any key when ready
```

In addition, if DOS cannot find the Command.com file, the following message is displayed:

Bad or missing Command Interpreter

6. Type **Y** and **<Enter>** to cause the DOS FORMAT program on the DOS floppy diskette to format the hard drive, which is designated 'C.' Format percentage completed is displayed until 100% is reached, then the **Format complete** message will appear and, after a pause, **System transferred**, followed by **Volume label (11 characters, Enter for none)?**

7. All disks can be labeled, as volumes of books can be named, and DOS provides up to 11 characters for this name. If a volume label is desired, type in the chosen name at this point and then **<Enter>**; otherwise just **<Enter>**. Next, the following appears with the x's shown on this page representing actual numbers on the screen—numbers that vary according to disk size.

```
xxxxxx      bytes total diskspace
xxxx        bytes used by system
xxx         bytes in bad sectors
xxxxxx      bytes available on disk

xxx         bytes in each allocation unit
xxx         allocation units available on disk

Volume Serial Number is xxx xxx
```

Disks that hold the system files are given a serial number by DOS.

If you partitioned your drive for any reason, each partition must be formatted and will become known by the next following letter, i.e., D, E, F, etc.

8. If you are uncertain about how to prepare your new hard disk drive for efficient computing operations, proceed to the next section.

DIRECTORIES AND FILES

If DOS directory and file structures are new to you, the following summary may be useful; otherwise, proceed to the subsections later in this section titled LOADING THE DOS FILES, CREATING A

CONFIG.SYS FILE, and CREATING AN AUTOEXEC.BAT FILE. This summary includes hands-on practice at making directories, which you perform in the steps that follow. In order to clarify the exercise, with your PC still booted off the DOS floppy diskette, you must execute a command which causes the name of the current, or active, directory to be displayed after the drive prompt. When you have done this, your A> prompt will simply change to A:\> at this stage, with the backslash indicating the current directory, in this case the "root" directory of A.

1. Type the command **PROMPT PG <Enter>** and observe the change to the prompt.

DOS organizes files on a hard disk to make them easy to find, just as files in a good filing cabinet system can be found. The file storage system, shown in Figure 4-3/1, is broken down as follows:

First level - Files and/or Directories
Second level - Files and/or Subdirectories
Third level - Files and/or Subsubdirectories

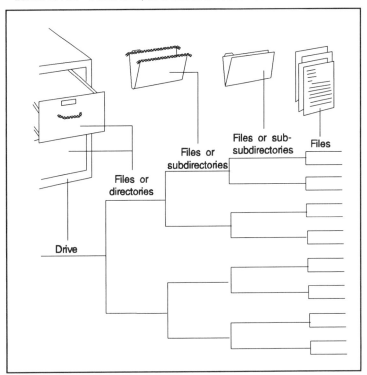

Figure 4-3/1—Typical Filing System

173

The directory structure can continue with ever-growing subdirectories, although this can become cumbersome and it is usually better to split the subject at the directory level. For example, instead of one STAFF directory, add SALES and PLANT subdirectories.

A directory can be created on a floppy diskette or hard disk drive, and the first level directories are made at the root prompt. To make a directory on your hard disk drive you must make that drive active.

2. At the A:\> type **C: <Enter>** and observe the prompt change to C:\>.

A directory is made by typing MD (MD means "Make directory"), followed by a space and then the name of the directory (no more than 8 characters in length).

3. For practice, make a SALES directory from the C:\> prompt by typing **MD SALES <Enter>**.

4. Change into that directory from the C:\> prompt by typing **CD\SALES <Enter>** (CD means "change directory"). The prompt should now read C:\SALES>.

5. Make a second level FIELD subdirectory at the C:\SALES> prompt by typing **MD FIELD <Enter>**, then enter that directory by typing **CD FIELD <Enter>**.

NOTE

When moving from a directory to one of its subdirectories, a space must be substituted for the backslash. However, if the move is directly from C:\> to the Field subdirectory, then the command would be CD\STAFF\FIELD.

A directory or subdirectory may be removed, but it must be empty of files. The command is best given at the level above the subdirectory to be removed, although it can be made from the C root by including the full path in the command.

6. Remove the FIELD subdirectory at the C:\SALES> prompt by typing **CD\ <Enter>** followed by **RD FIELD <Enter>** (RD is a DOS command for "remove directory").

7. Type **C: <Enter>** to change to the C:\> prompt, and then remove the SALES directory by typing **RD SALES <Enter>**.

A file can be created from the keyboard at any prompt using the DOS COPY CON command, although most files are created automatically from within application programs when text or data needs to be saved. A filename may not consist of more than 8 characters, and there are some DOS restricted characters such as * and : and ; (the allowable characters are letters of the alphabet, numbers, and ~ ! @ # $ % ^ & ( ) - _ { } '). Although not essential, filenames are usually followed by a period and a descriptive 3-letter extension such as .SYS for system, .EXE for executable, or .TXT for text. Application programs such as word processors, databases, and graphics, usually append their own extension automatically.

A file may be deleted by typing the DOS command DEL, followed by filename and extension, and then pressing Enter. However, it is necessary to be in the directory where the file resides, unless the path is included with the filename.

LOADING THE DOS FILES

Although at this stage your PC will boot off the hard disk because the system files are there, it has very limited capabilities. With those versions of DOS that include the DOS SHELL, such as 5.0 and 6.0, you invoke SETUP on the first diskette and loading is completed automatically. For earlier versions, the first step to improve the situation is to create a DOS directory on the computer's hard disk to hold all the DOS files that are on the DOS floppy disks. You do this in the steps that follow.

1. Type **MD DOS <Enter>** at the C:\> prompt.

2. Type **CD\DOS <Enter>** to enter the new DOS directory.

3. Place the first DOS diskette into A drive and type at the C:\DOS> prompt **COPY A:*.*** (an asterisk is a DOS wild card; thus, in essence, the command means regardless of name and extension, copy to the DOS directory all files that are on the diskette in drive A).

As the files are copied they are displayed by name on the screen, and when they are all copied the screen displays the number of files copied.

4. Repeat the procedure until all the DOS floppy diskettes have been copied to the hard disk.

175

CREATING A CONFIG.SYS FILE

The CONFIG.SYS (configuration system) file instructs DOS on how to configure the operating system when the computer is booted. The size of this file depends largely on the number and complexity of the application programs to be run. It can load device drivers, set the number of DOS buffers, specify the number of file handles, and more.

A device driver is a memory resident program required by DOS for devices that DOS does not recognize automatically, such as mice or extended memory. A buffer is a segment of memory that temporarily stores data while it is being transferred from one device to another. File handles control the number of files DOS can have open at one time.

Files may be created from the keyboard (console) by using the DOS COPY CON command. In the steps that follow you create a CONFIG.SYS file containing FILES and BUFFER commands.

1. At the C:\> prompt type **CD\ <Enter> COPY CON CONFIG.SYS <Enter> BUFFERS=15 <Enter> FILES=15 <Enter> F6 <Enter>**.

The CD\ command changes the directory from DOS, which was the active directory, to the C root, which is where the new file must reside. The F6 command at the end creates a ^Z (end-of-file marker) to which DOS responds with **1 File(s) copied.** As an alternative to F6, the key combination Ctrl+Z may be used.

CREATING AN AUTOEXEC.BAT FILE

The AUTOEXEC.BAT (automatic execution batch) file executes a series of DOS commands each time your PC is booted in order to save you from having to type them in each time. Two such commands that are very useful are PG, which you have already experienced, and PATH.

In most cases DOS is unable to leapfrog from one directory to another in search of a file. PATH specifies the names of directories, enabling DOS to search in those directories. For example, if certain DOS commands are typed at the C> or C:\> prompt with the DOS directory not in the path, the screen response will be **Bad command or file name,** and to execute the command the user must change to the DOS directory and repeat the command. In the steps that follow you make an AUTOEXEC.BAT file.

1. Type **CD\ <Enter> COPY CON AUTOEXEC.BAT <Enter> ECHO OFF <Enter> CLS <Enter> PROMPT PG <Enter> PATH C:\;C:\DOS <Enter> F6 <Enter>**.

The DOS ECHO OFF inhibits the display of DOS command names. CLS erases the contents of the screen. With the PATH command, entries must be exactly as shown, and if new directories are subsequently added, their exact name must be preceded by ;C:\ with no spaces. F6 causes DOS to respond with **1 File(s) copied**.

For a detailed explanation of the ECHO command and others that are difficult to understand, refer to your DOS user manual.

When loading software application programs, directories may need to be set up, and entries may have to be made in either the CONFIG.SYS file or the AUTOEXEC.BAT or both. Frequently, the software will do this automatically, but on other occasions the installation instructions will direct the user to do it manually, using either your DOS line or text editor, a utility program text editor, or a word processing program (in which case the file must be saved as an unformatted or ASCII file).

NOTE

When either a Config.sys or an Autoexec.bat file is first created, or at any subsequent time when they are edited, your PC must be rebooted to make the files or the changes become effective. The warm boot which is carried out by pressing Ctrl+Alt+Del is acceptable, as is pressing the Reset button on the computer control panel, or by switching off and on (the cold boot). In the latter case wait for 30 seconds before switching on again to allow electrical charges to drain from all electronic devices in your PC.

2. Press **Ctrl+Alt+Del** to make the changes effective and as a test to ensure that your PC boots off your new hard disk drive.

Section 4-4

UPGRADING AN XT TO AN AT-286, 386, OR 486

It is assumed for the purpose of this section that you have a turbo XT fitted with one 360K floppy disk drive, a hard disk drive, and a monochrome monitor with a Hercules-compatible video adapter card. Your plan is to retain your PC case, keyboard, floppy disk drive, hard disk drive, monitor, and video adapter card, to upgrade the other components, and to add a high density disk drive.

COMPONENTS AND PARTS TO ORDER

- Your choice of motherboard
- The required amount of memory of the correct specification for the motherboard
- Power supply to suit both the motherboard and your old case
- High density floppy disk drive with drive clamps, rails and, if necessary, a 5.25-inch/3.50-inch adapter
- Floppy/hard disk drive controller to suit your old hard drive

COMPONENT REMOVAL

Before disassembling your computer, back up your hard disk drive. With your PC open and disconnected from a power source after following the disassembly instructions in Section 2-4, perform the steps that follow to remove components that are to be upgraded.

1. Orient the computer case so that the left side is toward the front of the work table. Disconnect any internal cables attached to adapter cards, labeling them for subsequent ease of recognition.

2. Remove the end locking screws from all cards and store in a safe place.

3. Grasp a solid part of a card firmly between thumb and fingers, avoiding sharp wire ends on the back and fragile devices on the front, then withdraw it. Repeat for all cards and place them in a safe place, labeled for later identification if necessary.

4. Disconnect the 4-pin power supply cable and the 34-pin ribbon cable from the rear of the floppy disk drive.

5. Remove the clamps from the front of the drive bay that lock the drive into the bay, retaining them for when you replace the drive.

6. Slide the drive out of the bay on its rails and set it to one side.

7. Disconnect the 4-pin power cable from the hard disk drive.

8. Although not essential but in order to keep the work area uncluttered, disconnect the ribbon cables from the hard disk drive, label them, and store them for subsequent replacement.

9. Disconnect the power supply cables from the motherboard.

TIP Most power supply connectors have a centrally located plastic spring clip on one side of the connector which must be eased away from the socket on the motherboard before you can disconnect.

10. If you are using an external CMOS support battery attached to the power supply, disconnect it from the motherboard and remove it off the power supply.

11. Remove the screws from the back panel of your PC's chassis where they lock the power supply in position. Store them in a safe place.

12. Slide the power supply away from the back of the chassis until the tongue and slot locking device on the bottom of the power supply is released and the unit can be removed.

13. Disconnect the control panel cables from the motherboard.

14. Remove the screws from the metal hex posts which will not be visible until the motherboard is removed. (These posts were previously illustrated at Figure 2-9/1). Place the screws in a safe place—you will need them for the new board.

179

15. While facing the left-hand side of the computer case, slide the board toward you until it will lift out.

TIP Most likely you will not find step 15 easy to achieve because the plastic stand-offs tend to snag. Try jiggling the board until it moves to the necessary position for lifting off. As a last resort, squeeze the expanding arms of the plastic stand-offs and ease the board off them one at a time.

INSTALLING THE UPGRADE COMPONENTS

The first steps that follow, populating the memory banks, are carried out before the motherboard is installed in order to simplify matters. If the board is installed first there may well be drive bay hardware or other impediments that make memory installation difficult.

DIP Chips

1. Generally, new DIP chips tend to have the two rows of pins spread too wide to easily enter the slots in the socket. The purpose of this is so that when a chip is pushed into the mouth of a memory chip inserter, the pins are all bent inwards slightly, thereby applying pressure to the inner sides of the inserter to prevent the chip from falling out. To insert a chip by hand, you must first close the pins slightly by performing the sub-steps that follow.

    a. Firmly hold the chip at each end between thumb and forefinger.

    b. Place one row of pins flat on a hard surface, then apply some pressure to cause the whole row of pins to bend slightly inwards.

    c. Repeat for the other side.

TIP Do not overdo this modification; only a degree or two of angular bend is required and it is best to carry out the procedure in small steps, checking the pin positions against sockets after each bend.

2. When inserting a DIP chip by tool or by hand, align the notches in the chip and the socket, then ensure that the pins are lined up with the slots in the socket.

3. Ease the pins at the notch end just into the socket, then slowly rotate the chip backwards so that the other pins engage in the socket slots. Next, confirm that the pins are properly located, then apply steady but gentle pressure until the chip is firmly home.

TIP If at any time real resistance is felt, remove the chip and try again. If continued difficulty is experienced, recheck the alignment of pins to socket holes. If the difficulty persists, try another chip; this often works and most times you will find the offending chip will insert easily into another socket position.

4. Repeat steps 1 through 3 for all chips you are inserting.

5. Check all chips for proper insertion using a strong light and, preferably, a magnifying glass.

6. In the event of locating a chip with a bent pin, remove the chip and carefully straighten the pin using fine-nosed pliers, then reinsert taking extreme care to ensure that the damaged pin enters its slot properly.

SIMM and SIP Modules

1. Align the notches in module and socket, then use a thin-bladed screwdriver to hold back the plastic spring clip at the notch end of the socket and, while holding back the clip, insert the module pins into the socket slots, leaning the module slightly forward as you do it.

2. Ensure that all the pins are in their slots, then apply firm downward pressure as you bring the module to the vertical. When the module is properly seated, the clip, when released, should spring into its locking position.

3. Following population, check carefully under a strong light, using a magnifying glass if available, to ensure that each module is properly inserted and, in the case of SIP type RAM chips, that none of the pins are bent.

Motherboard

1. Hold the new motherboard so that the expansion slots are to the left. Next, offer the motherboard to the case and identify the best positions for the locations of the metal hex posts and insertion of the plastic stand-off supports.

2. If necessary, reposition the metal hex posts, using pliers to loosen them so that they will screw out of the chassis.

3. Insert the plastic supports into the motherboard (see Figures 1-2/3 and 1-2/4 in Section 1-2).

4. Refer to the user manual that came with the motherboard and set all jumpers and/or dipswitches to conform to the chosen computer configuration.

5. Position the motherboard just above the raised base plate of case, about half an inch back from the ultimate position, then lower it so that the plastic stand-offs drop into the wide parts of the slots in the base plate. Work the board forward until the threaded holes of the metal hex posts can be seen through the appropriate holes in the motherboard. When the board is correctly located the keyboard interface will be lined up accurately with the round hole in the back wall of the case. Using a Phillips screwdriver, secure the board in position with the screws from the old board.

6. Identify the jumpers and connectors that will interface the speaker and the control panel LEDs and buttons to the motherboard. Refer to the motherboard user manual for guidance.

7. Trace the control panel cables from their source to identify them, then interface them with the correct jumpers on the motherboard. Tidy up the cables, securing them with a tie or rubber band as necessary to ensure they are unlikely to become fouled up with other components.

Power Supply

1. If there is a voltage switch on your new power supply, make sure it is set correctly, then position the power supply so that you can slide the slot in the unit's base over the raised tongue on the computer chassis.

2. Secure the unit to the back of the computer chassis using the screws removed from the old power supply.

3. Identify the power supply connector with an orange cable at one end. Grip the connector so that the orange cable is nearest the back wall of the computer chassis and so that the connector itself is immediately above the end of the ribbon connector socket nearest the back wall of the computer case. See Figure 1-2/10 in Section 1-2.

4. Tilt the top of the connector away from the power supply and engage the pegs on the connector with the small slots in the socket. Rotate the connector back into a vertical position while pressing down to complete a secure interface. Repeat procedure for second connector.

Floppy Disk Drives

1. If a terminating resistor is installed on your new floppy disk drive, leave it in place since the drive is to be the first drive.

2. If necessary, install the drive into the 3.5-inch/5.25-inch adapter that came with the drive.

3. Fit rails to the drive or to the adapter.

4. Slide the drive along the drive bay rail guides of the top bay, and then secure it in position with the drive clamps that came with the new drive.

5. Interface to the back of the drive a 4-pin power supply cable, and the last connector on the 34-pin floppy drive controller ribbon cable.

6. Remove the terminating resistor on your old drive and then insert the drive into the next lowest bay, securing it with the old clamps.

7. Interface to the back of the drive a 4-pin power supply cable and the second connector on the 34-pin floppy drive controller ribbon cable.

Floppy/Hard Disk Controller Card

1. Insert your new hard/floppy disk controller card into a slot of the correct size, i.e., if you purchased a 16-bit card, locate it in a 16-bit slot, then screw it to the chassis back plate.

2. Interface the hard disk drive activity LED light cable (the jumpers are usually at the top front end of the card).

3. Interface the floppy disk drive ribbon cable to the card and replace the hard disk drive ribbon cables you temporarily removed, interfacing them to the correct sockets on the card and drive. See Figures 1-2/12 and 1-2/19 in Section 1-2.

Final Assembly

1. Interface the new keyboard, ensuring it is set to AT if it is switchable.

2. Replace your video adapter card and make the necessary connections to your monitor.

3. Remove any tools and debris from your PC and the surrounding area, then check all cable and card connections.

4. Connect the power cable from your surge protector (or wall outlet) to the new power supply.

Powering Up

1. Study the user manual for the new motherboard until you are fully conversant with setup procedures. A typical setup program is illustrated at Figure 2-2/2 in Section 2-2.

2. Insert a DOS boot diskette into your new floppy disk drive and power up.

3. Enter setup and record the new system configuration, i.e., RAM (usually automatic), floppy disk drives, and hard disk drive.

4. Unless your new hard disk drive has an IDE interface, initialize it by following the procedures in Section 4-3.

5. Format the drive, following, if necessary, the procedures in Section 4-3.

6. If your new system is operating correctly, power down, replace any remaining adapter cards, make any necessary interfaces to them, and then replace the cover of the PC.

If necessary, refer to Section 2-14 for reassembly procedures.

7. Restore the files you backed up.

8. If your new system is not functioning correctly, follow the appropriate problem and response procedures given in previous sections.

Section 4-5

UPGRADING AN AT-286 TO AN AT-386 OR 486

Basically, this is the easiest major upgrade since only the motherboard is involved. However, you will not gain much in overall operating speed if your old system has a slow hard disk with an 8-bit controller and a slow video card. Here are some numbers. First of all, if you are using an 8-bit disk controller card, the odds are that your hard disk is interleaved at 1:3, and if it is an old, slow disk, the access time may be in the order of 150 ms and the data transfer rate only 100K per second. With a new hard disk drive and controller of the right specifications, you can interleave 1:1 and increase those numbers to the order of 28 ms access time and over 200K per second data transfer rate. Next, if you are using a VGA monitor with an 8-bit video card fitted with slow memory, what you gain in the CPU you lose on the screen. Go for a 16-bit card with plenty of fast memory, and to speed it up even more, use a software program that remaps video ROM memory. Quarterdeck has a memory manager program that can manipulate video ROM and system RAM to speed up screen paint and refresh time by about 50%.

Logically, therefore, if you have an overall slow system and you plan to upgrade to 386 or 486, you should also upgrade the other slow components. It is assumed for the purpose of this section that you plan to upgrade your motherboard, memory, hard disk drive and controller, and video card.

COMPONENTS AND PARTS TO ORDER

- Your choice of motherboard
- The required amount of memory of the correct specification for the motherboard
- Hard disk drive of your choice, preferably one with at least 30 ms access time
- If necessary, a 5.25-inch/3.50-inch disk drive adapter
- A 16-bit floppy/hard disk drive controller to suit your new hard disk drive
- A 16-bit video card with fast installed memory

COMPONENT REMOVAL

Before disassembling your computer, back up your hard disk drive.

With your PC open and disconnected from a power source after following the disassembly instructions in Section 2-4, perform the steps that follow to remove components that are to be upgraded.

1. Orient the computer case so that the left side is toward the front of the work table. Disconnect any internal cables attached to adapter cards, labeling them for subsequent ease of recognition.
2. Remove the end locking screws from all cards and store in a safe place.
3. Grasp a solid part of a card firmly between thumb and fingers, avoiding sharp wire ends on one side and fragile devices on the other, then withdraw it. Repeat for all cards and place them in a safe place, labeled for later identification if necessary.
4. Disconnect the 4-pin power supply cable and the 20- and 34-pin ribbon cables from their interfaces at the rear of the old hard disk drive.
5. Remove the clamps from the front of the drive bay that lock the drive into the bay, retaining them for the replacement drive.
6. Slide the drive out of the bay on its rails.
7. Remove the rails and/or the 3.5" adapter from the drive, retaining them for the replacement drive.
8. Disconnect the power supply cables from the motherboard.

TIP Most power supply connectors have a centrally located plastic spring clip on one side of the connector which must be eased away from the socket on the motherboard before you can disconnect.

9. If you are using an external CMOS support battery, disconnect it from the motherboard and set it aside. It may be again useful at some future date.

10. Disconnect the control panel cables from the motherboard.

11. Remove the screws from the metal hex posts (these posts, previously illustrated in Figure 2-9/1, will not be visible until the motherboard is removed). Place the screws in a safe place—you will need them for the new board.

12. While facing the left-hand side of the computer case, slide the board toward you until it will lift out.

TIP Most likely you will not find step 12 easy to achieve because the plastic stand-offs tend to snag. Try jiggling the board until it moves to the necessary position for lifting off. As a last resort you might try pinching the expanding arms of a plastic stand-off and then pulling that part of the motherboard up and over the standoff, then repeat for the other stand-offs.

INSTALLING THE UPGRADE COMPONENTS

The first step that follows, populating the memory banks, is carried out before the motherboard is installed in order to simplify matters. If the board is installed first, there may well be drive bay hardware, or other impediments, that make memory installation difficult.

DIP Chips

1. Generally, new DIP chips tend to have the two rows of pins spread too widely to easily enter the slots in the socket. The purpose of this is so that when a chip is pushed into the mouth of a memory chip inserter, the pins are all bent inwards slightly, thereby applying pressure to the inner sides of the inserter to prevent the chip from falling out. To insert a chip by hand, you must first close the pins slightly by performing the sub-steps that follow.

   a. Firmly hold the chip at each end between thumb and forefinger.

   b. Place one row of pins flat on a hard surface, then apply some pressure to cause the whole row of pins to bend slightly inwards.

   c. Repeat for the other side.

TIP Do not overdo this modification; only a degree or two of angular bend is required, and it is best to carry out the procedure in small steps, checking the pin positions against sockets after each bend.

2. When inserting a DIP chip by tool or by hand, align the notches in the chip and the socket, then ensure that the pins are lined up with the slots in the socket.

3. Ease the pins at the notch end just into the socket, then slowly rotate the chip backwards so that the other pins engage in the socket slots. Next, confirm that the pins are properly located, then apply steady but gentle pressure until the chip is firmly home.

TIP If at any time real resistance is felt, remove the chip and try again. If continued difficulty is experienced, recheck the alignment of pins to socket holes. If the difficulty persists, try another chip; this often works and most times you will find the offending chip will insert easily into another socket position.

4. Repeat steps 1 through 3 for all chips you are inserting.

5. Check all chips for proper insertion using a strong light and, preferably, a magnifying glass.

6. Should you locate a chip with a bent pin, remove the chip and carefully straighten the pin using fine-nosed pliers, then reinsert taking extreme care to ensure that the damaged pin enters its slot properly.

SIMM and SIP Modules

1. Align the notches in module and socket, then use a thin-bladed screwdriver to hold back the plastic spring clip at the notch end of the socket, and while holding back the clip, insert the module pins into the socket slots, leaning the module slightly forward as you do it.

2. Ensure that all the pins are in their slots, then apply firm downward pressure as you bring the module to the vertical. When the module is properly seated, the clip, when released, should spring into its locking position.

3. Following population, check carefully under a strong light, using a magnifying glass if available, to ensure that each module is properly inserted and, in the case of SIP type RAM chips, that none of the pins are bent.

Motherboard

1. Hold the new motherboard so that the expansion slots are to the left. Next, offer the motherboard to the case and identify the best positions for the locations of the metal hex posts and the insertion of the plastic stand-off supports. See Figure 2-9/1.

2. If necessary, reposition the metal hex posts, using pliers to loosen them so that they will screw out of the chassis.

3. Insert the plastic supports into the motherboard (see Figures 1-2/3 and 1-2/4 in Section 1-2).

4. Refer to the user manual that came with the motherboard and set all jumpers and/or dipswitches to conform to the chosen computer configuration.

5. Position motherboard just above raised base plate of case, about half an inch back from the ultimate position, then lower it so that the plastic stand-offs drop into the wide parts of the slots in the base plate. Work the board forward until the threaded holes of the metal hex posts can be seen through the appropriate holes in the motherboard. When the board is correctly located, the keyboard interface will be lined up accurately with the round hole in the back wall of the case. Using a Phillips screwdriver, secure the board in position with the screws from the old board.

6. Identify the jumpers and connectors that will interface the speaker and the control panel LEDs and buttons to the motherboard. Refer to the motherboard user manual for guidance.

7. Trace the control panel cables from their source to identify them, then interface them with the correct jumpers on the motherboard. Tidy up the cables, securing them with a tie or rubber band as necessary to ensure they are unlikely to become fouled up with other components.

8. Identify the power supply connector with an orange cable at one end. Grip the connector so that the orange cable is nearest the back wall of the computer chassis and so that the connector itself is immediately above the end of the ribbon connector socket nearest the back wall of the computer case. See Figure 1-2/10 in Section 1-2.

9. Tilt the top of the connector away from the power supply and engage pegs on the connector with the small slots in the socket. Straighten the connector while pressing down to complete a secure interface. Repeat procedure for second connector.

Hard Disk Drive

1. Fit to your new drive the rails and/or the 5.25" adapter and rails that you removed from your old hard disk drive.

2. Slide the drive into the bay along the drive bay rail guides, and then secure it in position with the drive clamps you reserved after removing the old drive.

3. Connect to your new hard drive a 4-pin power supply cable and the 20-pin and 34-pin ribbon cables from your old drive.

4. Insert your new hard/floppy disk controller card into a 16-bit slot near the drive bays, then screw it to the chassis back plate.

5. Interface the ribbon cables from your new hard disk drive to the correct sockets on the card. See Figures 1-2/12 and 1-2/19 in Section 1-2.

Video Adapter Card

1. Set any switches and jumpers on the new card to suit your monitor, referring to the card's user manual for guidance.

2. Install the new card into a 16-bit slot and make the necessary connections to your monitor.

Final Assembly

1. Ensure that the keyboard is connected.

2. Remove any tools and debris from your PC and the surrounding area, then check all cable and card connections.

3. Ensure that the power cable from your surge protector (or wall outlet) is connected to the power supply.

Powering Up

1. Study the user manual for the new motherboard until you are fully conversant with setup procedures. A typical setup program is illustrated at Figure 2-2/2 in Section 2-2.

2. Insert a DOS boot diskette into your new floppy disk drive and power up.

3. Enter setup and record the new system configuration, i.e., RAM (usually automatic), hard disk drive, and video.

4. Unless your new hard disk drive has an IDE interface, initialize it by following the procedures in Section 4-3.

5. Format the drive, following, if necessary, the procedures in Section 4-3.

6. If your new system is operating correctly, power down, replace any remaining adapter cards, make any necessary interfaces to them, and then replace the cover of the PC.

If necessary, refer to Section 2-14 for reassembly procedures.

7. Restore the files you backed up.

8. If your new system is not functioning correctly, follow the appropriate problem and response procedures given in previous sections.

Section 4-6

CONFIGURING AN UPGRADED SYSTEM

OVERVIEW

Any good computer consultant will commence his session with a new client by asking the question, "What is the application?" In other words, what tasks will you expect your computer system to accomplish, and how fast will you want them accomplished. The answers to these questions lead to the types of software application programs and peripheral hardware that are available to accomplish the tasks. A decision on which specific programs to acquire will be based on the complexity of each task. For example, a $75.00 accounting program may be adequate for a private business with a staff of three but totally inadequate for a major corporation with hundreds of employees. Similarly, a dot matrix printer and a 12-inch monochrome monitor may be OK for private correspondence but inadequate for desktop publishing, which, ideally, requires a laser printer and a larger color monitor.

As soon as you have determined what software you plan to run, configuring your system becomes relatively straightforward. However, since you are possibly about to involve yourself in some serious expenditure, be sure in your own mind that you will not be looking for another upgrade next year. Price differentials between the hard disk drive you have in mind and one half as large again are not great, and the same is true for CPU speed increase from 25MHz to 33MHz. If you have a business, your business should grow and you will benefit from the upgrade. If your business does not grow, you may decide to sell it, and then your upgraded computer will attract more buyers. If you are a private user, you can just about that you will be demanding more and more from your system as the years roll by.

As a general rule, whenever you upgrade your computer system you should aim for capabilities well in excess of what you think you will need. However, since only you know what your future application is likely to be, only you or a consultant can come up with a final configuration.

BUYING CONSIDERATIONS

KEYBOARD Logically, you should upgrade to the 101-key type and gain the advantages of good function key layout and a separate numerical pad. Keyboards are inexpensive and, in the lower range, makes such as that put out by the keyboard division of Honeywell, Inc., are very adequate. Nevertheless, if you are a heavy keyboard user with preferences, you should try out a keyboard before making your decision.

MONITOR As well as for the all-important aspect of having the right monitor for the job, you should give equal consideration to your eyes and, possibly, other physical attributes. Health problems that may occur as a result of the low-level emissions put out by a monitor are covered in Appendix D.

Price differences between monochrome and color monitors can be dramatic, and with color, prices skyrocket even higher with increased size and better resolution. Your budget may well be an overriding consideration, and whereas for CAD work a 25-inch color monitor with subsystem resolution capability of 2048 x 1538 may be approaching the ideal, you can get the job done on something less luxurious. Also keep in mind the fact that if color is not essential, you can effect great savings by using a VGA monochrome monitor (white, as against amber or green) and still obtain very high monitor resolutions.

Size can be misleading. The size reference is a diagonal measurement of the picture tube before it is installed in the monitor case. After installation the visible diagonal measurement is much less, and when an application program's screen is displayed, even less. For example, the diagonal display size on a 14-inch Hyundai VGA Mono with an application running is only 11 inches.

In order to avoid flicker, purchase a monitor that has vertical screen refresh rates of at least 70Hz.

VIDEO CARD   Video cards, major players in the efficiency of video subsystems, are available at prices which display as much variation as monitor prices. You pay very few dollars for a nongraphics monochrome card, but many hundreds of dollars for a card that will drive your color monitor very fast at very high resolution.

The video card buying decision depends on and follows your determination of the monitor you want. A mono-monitor to be used for no more than word processing will be well served with a basic nongraphics card. However, since price increase is not that much when you move up to a card with graphics capability, it may be worth your consideration—just in case you decide to use graphics one day. In most other cases you match the video card you plan to buy with the monitor you have decided on. For example, there is no gain in buying a video card capable of driving a monitor at 2048 x 1538 resolution if your monitor is capable of no more than 1024 x 768, unless you plan to upgrade your monitor at a later date.

The following is a list of features to check for when buying a video card.

- A vertical refresh rate of 70Hz or better
- Drivers on board for the software you plan to use
- Support for the resolution capability of your monitor
- Support for the number of colors you require. For example, an 8-bit card supports up to 256 colors, while a 24-bit card supports millions (16.7) of colors.
- Sufficient memory on the card to support the colors and resolution you plan to use

POWER SUPPLY   Your chief considerations when purchasing a power supply are output watts and physical compatibility with your PC's case. One other consideration is quality, and in that regard you must rely on your own judgment. Price is usually an indication of quality.

MEMORY When memory prices are relatively low, you buy the best and the fastest that your PC can handle; otherwise, you must buy to suit your budget. An example of "relatively low" is $75.00 for 1MB of 100 ns DIPs. SIMM modules are a little more expensive; however, since installation is very much easier than installation of DIP chips, they should be your choice providing your motherboard accepts them. Hence, a motherboard upgrade will be influenced by the type of memory it uses.

MOTHERBOARD Bearing in mind the last sentence of the previous paragraph, the following are your other buying considerations.

- Unless you feel you must have a 486 because of the heavy demands likely to be made on your PC, choose a 386 which is more than adequate for average needs. If price is a factor dictating a 286, do what you can to squeeze out a few more dollars for a 386SX because it is vastly superior to the 286: the 386 protected mode can address much larger segments of protected memory; also the 386 supports mode switching and DOS multitasking, and it provides memory paging.
- If your budget permits a 386 or a 486 and you do not need blinding speed, choose DX versions running at 33 MHz; they may be more reliable than faster models, and they are more efficient that SX models.
- Choose a motherboard that offers cache capability.
- Buy a brand name with which you are familiar. Unknown manufacturers may no longer be in business when the time comes for you to seek their technical support.

HARD DISK DRIVE Whether you are a power user or a home hacker, you will enjoy working with a fast hard disk drive, therefore buy the fastest you can afford. So far as size is concerned, consider something 50% larger than you think you will need, and from the manufacturer point of view, buy a brand name you recognize.

Physical size (i.e., 3.5-inch or 5.25-inch) is a matter of personal choice generally related to the space available inside your PC. At one time, the larger drive was considered to be more reliable, but these days one is likely to be as reliable as the other.

Finally, you must match the hard disk drive you buy with a suitable controller card.

195

HARD DISK CONTROLLER The controller provides the interface, or encoding scheme, that transfers data to and from your hard disk. With an IDE interface you benefit by avoiding the need to initialize, and since the IDE controller card is less than half the size of most controller cards, it is inexpensive. ESDI and SCSI tend to transfer data faster than others, and that can be an attractive advantage. RLL packs 50% more data on a disk—highly desirable but possibly unreliable unless you carefully match drive and controller and buy good quality.

FLOPPY DISK DRIVE Since you are upgrading, your choice will be high density and your decision will be whether to buy 3.5-inch or 5.25-inch. Your usage of floppy diskettes should provide the answer, although with the relatively low prices of floppy drives you will always find one of each size convenient to have.

Appendix A

PRICES

Because readers will not all have access to the same supply source of computer components and because prices that are current at the time this book was written may differ greatly from those prevailing at the time you are reading this book, no attempt has been made to include prices. However, because pricing may be important to you in making a repair or upgrade decision, you are urged to obtain a recent copy of Computer Shopper (available at book stores) or other source of pricing and complete the blanks in this appendix. You should do this right after reading this book so that the information will be available to you when you have a problem and need to make the repair/upgrade decision.

After you have assembled price ranges, let your buying decision be influenced by the importance of the component. For example, the early failure of a low-cost mouse may not be a great inconvenience, whereas the early failure of a low cost power supply puts you out of action.

BARE-BONES SYSTEMS　　　　　PRICE RANGES IN U.S. $

AT286 __ MHz	_____	to	_____
AT386SX __ MHz	_____	to	_____
AT386DX __ MHz ___K cache	_____	to	_____
AT486DX __ MHz ___K cache	_____	to	_____

MOTHERBOARDS

AT286 __ MHz	_____	to	_____
AT386SX __ MHz	_____	to	_____
AT386DX __ MHz ___K cache	_____	to	_____
AT486DX __ MHz ___K cache	_____	to	_____

MEMORY

DIP ___ bit ___ ns   _____   to   _____
DIP ___ bit ___ ns   _____   to   _____
SIP ___ bit ___ ns   _____   to   _____
SIMM ___ bit ___ ns   _____   to   _____

CASES

Mini-desktop w/wo   _____   to   _____
  power supply
AT-style desktop w/wo   _____   to   _____
  power supply
Mini-tower w/wo power supply _____   to   _____
Full-tower w/wo power supply _____   to   _____

POWER SUPPLIES

150 watts (XT)   _____   to   _____
200 watts (AT)   _____   to   _____
250 watts   _____   to   _____
330 watt   _____   to   _____

FLOPPY DISK DRIVES

360K 5.25 inch   _____   to   _____
720K 3.50 inch*   _____   to   _____
1.2MB 5.25 inch   _____   to   _____
1.44MB 3.50 inch*   _____   to   _____
2.88MB 3.50 inch*   _____   to   _____

* With 3.50 inch/5.25 inch adapter

HARD DISK DRIVES

___ MB __ ns ___ interface   _____   to   _____
___ MB __ ns ___ interface   _____   to   _____

FLOPPY/HARD DISK DRIVE CONTROLLER

___ bit _____ interface   _____   to   _____

KEYBOARD

____ key, switchable/not switchable

_____ to _____

MOUSE

____ button, type _____ to _____

MONITOR

Color/mono, interlaced/non-interlaced,
_____ inch, _____ dot pitch, _____ to _____

VIDEO CARD

Hercules/VGA/Super VGA, _____K memory,
____ x ____ res, _____ colors _____ to _____

Appendix B
TYPICAL I/O ADDRESSES

Hex Address	Task	Task on Your PC
00 to 0F	DMA controller 8237 #1	_____
20 to 21	Interrupt controller #1	_____
40 to 43	8253 timer	_____
60 to 63	XT only peripherals	_____
60 to 64	AT only keyboard controller	_____
70 to 71	AT only CMOS RAM	_____
80 to 8F	DMA page registers	_____
A0 to A1	AT only interrupt controller	_____
A0 to AF	XT only NMI mask register	_____
C0 to DF	AT only DMA controller 8237 #2	_____
F0 to FF	AT only math coprocessor	_____
1F0 to 1F8	AT only hard disk controller	_____
200 to 20F	Games I/O	_____
210 to 217	XT only expansion	_____
238 to 23B	Bus mouse	_____
23C to 23F	Alternate bus mouse	_____
278 to 27F	Parallel printer port #2	_____
2F8 to 2FF	Serial port #2	_____
300 to 31F	Prototype card	_____
320 to 32F	XT only hard disk controller	_____
378 to 37F	Parallel printer port #1	_____
380 to 38F	Bysynch 2	_____
3A0 to 3AF	Bysynch 1	_____

Hex Address	Task	Task on Your PC
3BO to 3BF	Monochrome/printer adapter	_____
3BC to 3BF	Parallel printer port #3	_____
3D0 to 3DF	Color graphics adapter	_____
3FO to 3F7	Floppy disk drive controller	_____
3F8 to 3FF	Serial port #1	_____

Appendix C

SHAREWARE AND PUBLIC DOMAIN VENDORS AND ORGANIZATIONS

Association of Shareware Professionals
545 Grover Road
Muskegon, MI 49442

CompuServe Mail - ASP
Ombudsman 70007-3536

Brown Bag Software
P.O. Box 60000
San Francisco, CA 94160-1719

Tel: 1-408-559-4545

Generic Computer Systems
22612 Foothill Blvd #200C
Hayward, CA 94541

Tel: 1-510-581-1494

Most Significant Bits
13733B Madison Avenue
Lakewood, OH 44107

Tel: 1-800-755-4619

PC Shareware
P.O. Box 99226
San Diego, CA 92169

Tel: In San Diego 272-6673
     1-800-447-2181
Fax: 1-619-274-5837

Public Brand Software
P.O. Box 51315
Indianapolis, IN 46251

Tel: 1-800-426-3425

Softshoppe, Inc
P.O. Box 3678
Ann Arbor, MI 48106

Tel: 1-800-829-2378
Fax: 1-313-761-7639

Appendix D

MONITOR RADIATION

Most electrical gadgetry emits non-ionizing electromagnetic radiation ranging from the infinitesimal measurement associated with an electric shaver to the substantial output of a major high-voltage installation, but there is uncertainty about how harmful this radiation is.

Non-ionizing electromagnetic radiation is an invisible, omnipresent form of energy emitted by power lines, microwave ovens, TV sets, radio transmitters, radar, video display terminals (VDTs), and many other modern electrical devices.

During the last few years, controversy has raged as to whether there is a danger, and the hottest controversies have been fuelled by evidence from studies purported to show specific trends: increased risk of cancerous growths, fetal malformations, increased risk of miscarriage, slow intrauterine growth, increased incidences of brain tumors.

Dr. J. Phillips of the Cancer Therapy and Research Center, San Antonio, found that colon cancer cells subjected to electromagnetic fields tended to grow fast and last longer.

The findings of a 1981/82 study conducted at the Kaiser Permanente Medical Care Program in Oakland, California, on over 1,500 pregnant women was published by the American Journal of Industrial Medicine. The findings: of the 117 women who worked 20 or more hours on the VDT, 52 had miscarriages, roughly 44%.

Dr. Michele Marcus, assistant professor of epidemiology at Mt. Sinai School of Medicine in New York has reported on the higher incidence of miscarriage among VDT users.

NIOSH, the National Institute for Occupational Safety and Health, has reported that 81% of computer operators complain of eye strain.

Many worker organizations have called for legislation, and Suffolk County in New York was the first to respond, approving legislation that requires employers with 20 or more terminals to give VDT users 15-minute breaks every three hours and to offer health training. Twenty-five states have VDT bills in House. Some states, together with the District of Columbia, have formulated guidelines for government workers' use of VDTs.

Law suits and workmen's compensation cases are being settled in favor of the plaintiff, based on reasonable doubt and statistical link.

Filters are available which the makers claim reduce most of the very low frequency emissions (VLF) put out by the fly-back transformer that resides in every VDT, but a good one costs $60.00 and up, with another $15.00 or so for installation. Some monitor manufacturers have acknowledged the possibilty of health risk by building filters into their products.

Other known problems that suggest total ergonomic consideration is necessary if a user is associated with regular and prolonged computer/VDT operation are now listed.

- Vision problems regularly occur after 3 to 8 hours a day spent at a computer/VDT.
- The high level of concentration needed to efficiently address a computer/VDT leads to headaches.
- Musculosketal problems such as carpel tunnel syndrome and backache result from improper work station configuration and design.
- Even if not proven a health hazard, VLF emissions, electrostatic, and radiation create fear, which in itself can be a health hazard.

Glossary

10-pin ribbon cable	Cable that connects ports to an I/O card.
16-bit	Limits data path on a bus or adapter card to a width of 16 bits.
20-pin ribbon cable	Hard drive data cable.
32-bit	Limits data path on a bus or adapter card to a width of 32 bits.
34-pin ribbon cable	Hard or floppy drive controller cable.
386-enhanced mode	Creates "virtual" memory when used with 80386 CPUs and higher, and appropriate software.
8-bit	Limits data path on a bus or adapter card to a width of 8 bits.
Adapter card	A printed circuit card, or board, used to control and connect electronic devices to the mother-board.
Address	Location in memory for the storage of specific information.
Address bus	The wire path that carries addressing information to specify a location for data in memory.
Asyn 1 and Asyn 2	Asynchronous (as opposed to synchronized) communication ports.
AT	Advanced technology. Name given to a PC installed with an 80286 or higher CPU.
ATTRIB	DOS command that allows the attributes of a file to be changed.
Auto-parking	A technique on modern hard disk drives to prevent the read/write heads from touching the platters when a PC is not operating.
Back up	To copy data from one disk to another (or tape) as a safeguard in case the first disk loses its data.
Bare-bones	A partially built PC consisting of case, power supply, and motherboard.
Base plate	The bottom of a PC's case.

Battery	Maintains the configuration information in the CMOS chip in ATs when the PC is switched off.
Baud	Measurement of transmission speed for a modem and other devices. One bit per second equals one baud.
Bay	Receptacle in a PC for a disk drive.
Beep-code	Translation of the speaker signals transmitted by the BIOS.
Binary system	The counting system used by CPUs based on the numbers 0 and 1.
BIOS	Basic Input/Output System. Preprogrammed instructions that allow a PC to start operating when switched on.
Bit	The binary counting unit.
Bit-mapped	A character or graphic created from individual dots as against creation by outline.
Boot record	Starts the DOS boot process and defines disk characteristics.
Booting	The loading of the stages of DOS.
Bootstrap program	The program that starts the boot process.
Bus	Electrical interface between motherboard and adapter cards.
Bus-mouse	A mouse with its own adapter card.
Byte	Eight bits.
Cache	A cache of high speed memory, in addition to RAM, which can be used for fast data transfer.
CAD	Computer Aided Design. Application software specifically for design creation such as architectural or engineering drawings.
Cap	The shorting (switch) unit that "caps" jumper pins.
Capacitor	An electrical device that develops and holds a charge of electricity.
CGA	Color Graphics Adapter. A type of color monitor.
CHKDSK	DOS command that checks and reports on the condition of a disk.
Clock speed	The speed of the CPU in megahertz.

Clone	A copy of an IBM PC.
Cluster	A set of contiguous sectors.
CMOS	Complimentary Metal Oxide Semiconductor. A programmable chip for storing an AT's configuration.
COM1 or COM2	Communications ports 1 and 2. Also called serial ports.
COMMAND.COM	DOS command processor that executes internal and external commands.
COMMSPEC	A command telling DOS to find the COMMAND.COM file under a different name.
Compress	1. A technique for compressing files so that they occupy less space.
	2. A technique for defragmenting a disk.
CONFIG.SYS	A user-defined DOS system file that configures a PC's system.
Conflict	An error that occurs when two devices attempt to use the same system resources.
Connector	A "plug" on the end of a cable.
Control-panel	A switch panel with LED lights on the face of a PC used for controlling some features and indicating activity of others.
Controller	An adapter card that controls disk drives. Also used in the term "Video controller."
Conventional memory	The first 640 Kilobytes of RAM memory.
CPU	Central Processing Unit. The CPU is, in effect, the actual computing device in a PC.
Cross-linked files	Files with confused pointers which inhibit DOS from accessing them.
Cylinder	Tracks of the same DOS number on each hard disk platter.
Data bus	The path along which data is carried; eight bits at a time in an 8-bit bus, 16 bits in a 16-bit bus, etc.
Data encoding scheme	The formula used by a hard disk drive controller to define how a hard disk will read, write, and store data.

DEBUG	A DOS programming utility also used in conjunction with qualifiers for other activities such as XT hard disk initializing.
Device driver	A program that controls a device; a mouse for example.
Diagnostic program	1. A resident program in the BIOS of an AT that carries out self-diagnostics. 2. An application program for diagnosing faults.
Digitizing tablet	An input device consisting of a stylus and a sensitized board.
DIP chip	Dual Inline Package. The original type of memory chip that inserts into rows (banks) of sockets.
Dipswitches	Mini-switches used to set parameters.
Dirty electric current	Electric current from a wall outlet that fluctuates beyond the norm.
Disk crash	When the read/write heads of a hard disk are jarred into striking the platters.
Disk fragmentation	The separation of a file on a disk into several noncontiguous parts as a result of editing.
Disk protection	Practices and techniques that assist in preventing the occurrence of software problems.
Disk repair	The correction of software or formatting problems.
Disk utility program	A program specifically designed for data recovery and/or disk repair.
DMA channel	Direct Memory Access. A fast route for bypassing the CPU in the transfer of information when CPU involvement is not required.
DOS	Disk Operating System. A software interface between PC and user.
DOS kernel	The portion of DOS responsible for directory and file management and for interfacing with applications.
DOS sectors	Part of a track on a disk.

Dot pitch	The combined size of the red, green, and blue phosphor spots on the back of a monitor's screen stated in millimeters.
Dot matrix printer	A printer that creates type by striking an inked tape with varying numbers of pins.
DPI	Dots per inch. The number of dots in one square inch; used to specify screen, printer, or scanner resolution.
DRAM	Dynamic Random Accessible Memory. Same as RAM. The volatile memory created by memory chips when a PC is switched on; used for program instruction and temporary data storage.
Drive bay	See Bay.
Drive controller	See Controller
Drive-select jumper	Used to set numbering parameters on a disk drive.
EGA	Enhanced Graphics Adapter. A type of color monitor.
EISA	Extended Industry Standard Architecture. A bus design compatible with ISA but incorporating many of the MCA improvements.
Error messages	Messages relayed by speaker or by screen display.
ESDI	Enhanced Small Disk Interface. A data encoding scheme for hard disk drives.
Expanded memory	Memory above the 640K limited by versions of DOS preceding 5.0. See LIM.
Expansion slots	Receptacles in the bus for adapter cards.
Extended memory	Memory above 1MB in ATs not recognized by versions of DOS prior to 5.0.
FAT	File Allocation Table. Keeps track of file locations and clusters on a disk.
Formatting	Preparation of a disk to enable it to accept data.
Gigabytes (gb)	Approximately one thousand megabytes.
Graphics card	Video card that controls the display of computer-generated images.

Gray scale	The number of shades between black and white that can display on a monitor or be printed.
Hexadecimal	A numbering system that utilizes 0 through 9 and A through F.
I/O address	CPU memory address for each device in a PC.
IDE	Integrated Drive Electronics. A data encoding scheme for hard disk drives.
Initializing	Applying to a hard disk sets of fundamental parameters that relate to a specific type of controller.
Instruction	One step in a batch of steps that instructs the CPU to carry out a task
Interface	Physical connection.
Interleave	An interleave number specifies how data is read or written to the sectors of a hard disk, if necessary skipping sectors in order to correlate system and disk speed.
Interrupts	A technique for putting the system on hold in order to allow another operation to take place.
IRQ	One of a set number of lines necessary for an interrupt.
Jumper	A form of switch using pins that can be shorted by a cap to make a connection.
K	Kilobyte. 1024 bytes.
Keyboard BIOS	The brains of a keyboard that convert key action to signals recognizable by the CPU.
LED	Light Emitting Diode. A small light used to indicate activity such as disk usage.
LIM	Lotus-Intel-Microsoft Expanded Memory Specification. Allows the use of expanded memory.
Lost cluster	Inaccessible cluster caused by absence of the FAT pointer added when a file is written. Usually caused by system termination during an operation.
LPT	DOS reserved name for a parallel printer port.
Magnetic head	The read/write head on a disk drive.
MB	Megabyte. 1,048,576 bytes.

MCA	Micro Channel Architecture. An IBM bus design that uses nonstandard adapter cards but offers some improvements over standard architecture.
Memory chip	An electronic device that connects to the motherboard to provide RAM when a PC is operating.
Memory map	Schematic illustration of how a PC uses memory.
Memory modes	See Real mode, Protected mode, and 386 enhanced mode.
MFM	Modified Frequency Modulation. A data encoding scheme for hard disk drives.
MHz	Megahertz. One million cycles per second.
Micro-channel	See MCA.
Microprocessor	See CPU.
Mini-tower	A half-size tower case.
MIPS	Millions of instructions per second.
Mirror	A procedure that saves information about a disk to a special file, thereby enhancing any subsequent recovery action.
Motherboard	The main board of a PC on which is housed the CPU, memory, adapter slots, in addition to many other electronic devices.
Mouse	A peripheral device that displays a movable pointer on the monitor screen for creating graphics and activating commands.
MS-DOS	The Microsoft disk operating system.
Multi-I/O card	An adapter card providing ports such as printer, communications, and game.
Non-maskable interrupt	An interrupt that causes a message to be displayed on the screen.
Notch	An indentation on memory chips or modules and memory sockets to indicate correct installation direction.
OCR	Optical Character Recognition. A type of software that converts scanned type to editable text.

Parallel printer port	See LPT.
Parity	A technique for checking data errors.
Path statement	An instruction, usually in the AUTOEXEC.BAT file, that points DOS to specified directories.
Pen-mouse	A mouse shaped like a fat pen.
Peripheral	Any device external to a PC.
Pixel	One illuminated dot on a monitor screen.
Platter	One of several disks that make up a hard disk drive.
Port	A connector, usually on the part of an adapter card that is visible through the back plate of a PC.
Power supply	An internal component of a PC that steps down line power to that used by the PC.
Powering up	Switching on a PC.
Preventive maintenance	Precautions taken to help prevent failures.
Printer port	See LPT.
Protected mode	Extended memory that can be protected from interference by other memory using devices and programs.
Public domain	Unlicensed software.
Qualifier	An addition to a DOS command that adds to or changes the nature of the command.
Rails	Literally rails that fit to the sides of drives so that they can be slid along tracks into drive bays.
RAM	Random Accessible Memory. See DRAM.
Read/write head	See Magnetic head.
Real mode	The mode of operation of an 8088 CPU. Real mode is incorporated into 80286, 80386, and 80486 chips.
Resolution	See DPI.
Ribbon cables	Flat plastic cables with a number of embedded wires.
RLL	Run Length Limited. A data encoding scheme for hard disk drives.

ROM	Read Only Memory. Memory that has been preprogrammed and which a user can read but not write to.
RS-232	A standard for a type of serial cable.
SCSI	Small Computer System Interface. A data encoding scheme for hard disk drives.
Serial port	Same as COM1 or COM2.
Setup	A program in the BIOS of an AT where the PC's configuration can be entered.
Shareware	Software that can be used after paying a small fee to the author.
SIMM	Single Inline Memory Module. See module.
SIP	Single Inline Package. See module.
Solid state	Without moving parts.
Standard bus	The bus on original IBM PCs and most compatibles.
Storage capacity	The number of data bytes that can be stored on a disk.
Stylus	A form of pen-mouse used with a digitizing tablet.
Surge protector	A device that stabilizes fluctuations in line current.
Switchable keyboard	A keyboard that can be used with an XT or an AT.
SX	An 80386 CPU with only a 16-bit external data path.
Terminating resister	A scheme to allow a single ribbon cable to be used with either one or two drives.
Tower case	A tall, vertical PC case generally used with power machines such as network servers.
Track ball	A form of inverted mouse with the ball moved by hand.
Tracks	Concentric circles on a disk for storing data.
Turbo XT	An XT that can be switched between two CPU speeds.
Undelete	To use a utility to undelete an inadvertently deleted file.

Unformat	To use a utility to unformat an inadvertently formatted disk.
UPS	Uninterruptible Power Supply. An external device that, in the event of a power outage, automatically supplies battery power to a PC's power supply.
VGA	Video Graphics Array. A type of color monitor.
Video card	See Adapter card and Controller card.
Video subsystem	The monitor, video card, and some internal electronics such as IRQs.
Virtual memory	Portion of unallocated hard disk space used as a form of RAM.
Virus	Destructive software program which can be introduced automatically to a hard disk via a modem or a floppy diskette.
Wait-state	Delays introduced into a PC to match memory speed to hard disk speed. See also Interleave.

Index

16-bit data path, 7
32-bit data path, 7
8-bit data path, 7
80286 CPU, 5
80486 CPU, 5

Adapter card connectors, 33
Adapter card installation, 32
Adapter cards, 31-32, 126
   connectors, 33
   installation, 129
   removal, 129
Address bus, 7
Addressable memory, 7
AT, 4
AUTOEXEC.BAT file, 176

Bare-bones PC, 158
Beep codes, 72
Binary system, 6
BIOS, 14, 107
BIOS diagnostic checks, 72
Boot failure, 134
Buying considerations, 195

Cable connections, 23
   control panel, 23
   power supply, 23
Cables, 38, 131
   disk drive, 38
   exterior, 131
   hard disk interface, 39
Checkit, 65
CHKDSK, 119
Cleaning a floppy disk drives,
   114-115
Clusters, 57
CMOS, 15

Color monitors, 47
COM 1 or 2, 37
Component upgrade, 154
Components, 11
   BIOS, 14
   motherboard, 12
CONFIG.SYS file, 176
Configuration, 192
   application, 194
Conventional memory, 19
Covers (PCs), 89
CPU, 4, 15
   80286, 5
   80386, 5
   80486, 5
   speeds, 7
CPU Specifications, 5
CPU speeds, 7
Cylinders, 57

Data bus, 7
Data paths, 7
   8-bit data path, 7
   16-bit data path, 7
   32-bit data path, 7
Data recovery, 78
DEBUG program, 122
Diagnostics, 64
Digitizing boards, 139
Digitizing tablets, 45
DIP, 16
Dipswitches, 21
Disassembly, 86
   tools, 87
Disk drive controllers, 30
Disk fragmentation, 58
Disk protection, 79

Disk recovery, 78
    PC Tools, 66
Disk recovery services, 85
Disk repair, 83
    PC Tools, 66
Disk structure
    clusters, 57
    cylinders, 57
    fragmentation, 58
    sectors, 57
    tracks, 56
DMA channels, 34
DOS. See MS-DOS
DOS files, 173
Dot matrix printers, 48
Drive connectors, 40

ESDI, 29

Failed boot, 134
Failures overview, 8
Floppy disk drives, 26
    cleaning, 114
    controllers, 30
    drive-select jumper, 26
    installation, 115
    problems, 113
    removal, 115
    terminating resistor, 26
Formatting a hard disk, 123
Fragmentation, 58

Hard disk drives, 27
    cable interfaces, 39
    CHKDSK, 118
    controllers, 30
    initializing, 31, 122
    installation, 121
    interfaces
        ESDI, 29
        IDE, 29
        MFM, 29

RLL, 29
SCSI, 29
interleave specifications, 29
magnetic heads, 27
platters, 27
removal, 120
sizes, 28
Hard disk drive cable interfaces, 39
Hard disk initializing, 31, 122
Hardware failure symptoms, 73

I/O addresses, 34, 200
IBM-PC compatibility, 3
IDE, 29
Info+ diagnostics, 68
Initializing, 31, 122
        DOS DEBUG program, 122
        Proprietary programs, 122
Ink-jet printers, 49
Intel, 4
Interleave specifications, 29
Interrupts, 18
IRQ information for an AT, 34
IRQs, 34

Jumpers, 21

Keyboard BIOS chip, 15
Keyboards
    XT/AT switchable, 92

Laser printers, 48
LIM EMS, 20
Limitations of repair, 9
Low-level format. See
    Initializing
LPT1, 2, or 3, 37

MCA (micro-channel architecture), 3
Memory, 103
    addresses, 33, 126

banks, 16
chips, 15
DMA channels, 34
I/O addresses, 34
IRQs, 34
maps, 19
memory insertion, 105
memory removal, 105
modes, 19
  386-enhanced, 20
  protected, 20
  real, 20
DIP, 16
SIMM, 17
SIP, 17
types, 19
  conventional, 20
  expanded, 20
  extended, 20
MFM, 29
Mice, 43, 137
Microsoft diagnostic utility, 66
MIPS, 7
Modems, 50, 148
Monitors, 46
  how they work, 46
  resolution, 47
Motherboards, 12, 110
  locating and locking
    slots, 111
  plastic stand-off, 14
  removal, 109
  replacement, 110
MS-DOS, 51-52
  commands, 56
  disk structure, 56
  how it works, 52
Multi I/O cards, 36
  COM 1 or 2, 37
  LPT1, 2, or 3, 37

Non-Maskable Interrupt, 18

Operating system, 51
  MS-DOS, 51

PC development, 4
PC Tools, 66
Peripherals, 42
  digitizing tablets, 45
  keyboards, 42
  mice, 43
  monitors, 46
  scanners, 45
Pixel, 46
Planning an upgrade, 153
Platters, 56
Plotters, 49, 145
Power supply, 23, 99
  high voltage risk, 25
Printers, 48, 143
  dot matrix, 48
  impact, 48
  ink-jet printers, 49
  laser, 48
Problem solving DOS
  commands, 58
Proprietary programs, 80
Public domain software, 68

**RAM (Random Accessible
  Memory)**, 17
Real mode, 20
Reassembly (PCs), 133
Repair considerations, 10
Repair limitations, 9
RLL, 29

Scanners, 45, 141
SCSI, 29
Sectors, 57
Setting up a hard disk drive, 169
Setup programs, 75

SIMM, 17
SIP, 17
Software problem symptoms, 74
Speaker, 40
Standard bus, 13
Startup problems, 71
Static electricity, 88
Switches, 21
    dipswitches, 21
    jumpers, 21
SX, 6

Testing (PCs), 133
Types of personal computer, 3

Undelete, 81
Unformat, 82
UPS (Uniterruptible Power
    Supply), 23
Upgrade or bare-bones
    decision, 158

Upgrades, 153
    AT-286 to an AT-386
        or 486, 157
    AT-286 to an AT-386,
        or 486, 185
    disk controller card, 166
    floppy disk drive, 163
    hard disk drive, 164
    memory, 159
    power supply, 167
    video subsystem, 168
    XT to AT, 155
    XT to AT-286, 386,
        or 486, 178

Video cards, 35, 95
    Hercules, 35
    VGA, 36
Virtual protected memory
    mode, 20

XT, 4